Pierre-Marie Dumont

SPLENDORS OF CHRISTMAS

Father Frédéric Curnier-Laroche
Art Commentaries

MAGNIFICAT

Paris • New York • Oxford • Madrid

Cover and pages 4-5: **Francesco Botticini** (1446–1497), *The Virgin Adoring the Child Surrounded by Saint John the Baptist and Two Angels*, oil on wood, 32.3 in. diameter.

The work that greets us on the cover sums up in and of itself the purpose of this publication. It is firstly an invitation to a journey. Just as the path meanders in the background of the composition, leading the eye toward a city with its wide-stretched ramparts and imposing buildings, so this book carries us along through sacred history, in which the Savior is revealed. For the Florentine artist, this is the route that will later be taken by the newborn Son of God, leading him to the Holy City, in order that *"the Lord of hosts may reign on Mount Zion and in Jerusalem, glorious in the sight of his elders"* (cf. Is 24:23).

This book enables our meditation and contemplation of the mystery of the Incarnation. Following the example of this delicate and gentle Madonna, who serenely and soberly considers the Child lying at her feet, and this young angel who turns to look at us, we can open our hearts to the One who comes right to each one of us. This will be the news proclaimed by John the Baptist, whom Botticini presents here as a toddler already surrounded by symbols of his prophecy.

Everything in this work plunges us into the airy and subtle atmosphere of the Renaissance: the meticulous rendering of the landscape and its elements enhanced by a vaporous light, the velvety texture of the deep-colored garments, and the discreet transparency of Mary's veil, not to mention the idealized beauty of the subjects. Thus our meditation on these four persons recalls us to Charles Peguy's striking observation: "Creation was hanging on God's very word. Eternity itself was awaiting. Eternity itself was suspended."

Commentaries on two-page artwork can be found at the end of this volume, pages 120-124.

Publisher: Pierre-Marie Dumont

Under the direction of Romain Lizé, Vice President
Editor: Pauline Berthelé
Iconography: Isabelle Mascaras
Art Direction: Élisabeth Hebert, Elena Germain

Meditations: Pierre-Marie Dumont
Art Commentaries: Frédéric Curnier-Laroche

Translation: Janet Chevrier
Proofreading: Claire Gilligan
Production: Thierry Dubus, Sabine Marioni

ISBN: 978-1-936260-96-6
First edition: October 2014
© 2014 by Magnificat Inc., New York
All rights reserved.

TABLE OF CONTENTS

FOREWORD

Father Peter John Cameron, O.P.

ach Christmas, I observe a little custom. Of all the Christmas
cards that come in the mail, only those featuring an image of
the Madonna and Child are granted pride of place on the fire-
place mantel.

It amazes me to contemplate, year after year, the seemingly endless
variations on the sacred theme of Infant and Mother—one artist's depiction more beautiful than the next.

Why such fascination with this subject?

One answer is theological. The Catechism of the Catholic Church
speaks about the method by which the Church "aims to initiate people
into the mystery of Christ." That method proceeds "from the visible to
the invisible, from the sign to the thing signified" (1075). When we look
at a painting of God-made-flesh in the arms of Mary, we are led via the
eyes of faith into an unseen world of wonder and grace, more real than
anything around us.

This method is based on human experience. Saint Thomas Aquinas
observed how it is that the sight of a lovable object entices the beholder
to love it and to desire to enjoy it.[1] We need good things to be shown to
us in order for the magnetic force of those good things to draw us in. As
Pope Benedict XVI expressed it, "Knowledge of God is possible only
through the gift of God's love becoming visible."[2] Artistic renditions of
the splendors of Christmas act like sacramentals, enabling us to know
and desire and love God because of his Love made visible through Our
Lady.

And this gives us hope! In the Revelations of Bridget of Sweden, the
saint mystically hears the Blessed Virgin say: "When I was nursing my
Son, he was endowed with such great beauty that whoever looked upon
him was consoled and relieved of any sorrow he may have had in his
heart. And so, many people said one to another, 'Let us go to see Mary's
Son, that we may be consoled.'"

Yet, as consoling as it may be for us to gaze on portraits of Mother and
Baby, there is a greater gaze that transports us: that of God's gaze upon
us. Pope Francis reminds us that "in order to love life we don't need to fill
it up with things, which then become idols; we need only that Jesus watch
over us. It is his gaze that tells us: It is good that you are alive, your life
is not useless, because you have been entrusted with a great duty. This
is true wisdom: a new outlook on life that comes from encounter with
Jesus."[3] The splendors of Christmas, then, move us to put aside "all suspi-
cion or mistrust, and turn our gaze to what we are all seeking: the radiant
peace of God's face."[4]

1 ST I-II, 31, 6, 3.
2 *Jesus of Nazareth*, p. 194.
3 Address to participants in Rome's Diocesan Conference, Monday, June 16, 2014.
4 *Evangelii Gaudium*, #244.

LEX

MYSTERIVM IVSTIFICATIONIS

PECCATVM

MORS

ESAYAS PROPHETA
ECCE VIRGO CONCIPIET ET PARIET FILIVM . ISA

GRATIA

IVSTIFICATIO NOSTRA

INRI

HOMO

USER EGO HOMO,
VIS ME ERIPIET EX
OC CORPORE MORTI
OB NOXIO · RO.7

IOANNES BAPTISTA

ECCE AGNVS ILLE DEI QVI TOLLIT PECCATV MVDI. IO.1

THE LONG WAIT OF
THE PEOPLE
OF ISRAEL

From the root of Jesse a flower will blossom,
the glory of the Lord will fill the earth, and all creation shall see
the saving power of God.

Page 10: **Lucas Cranach the Elder** (1472–1553), *The Virgin in Prayer* (1540), right panel of the triptych of the Resurrection, oil on wood, 254.3 x 67.3 in.

How blest that Mother, in whose shrine/ The great Artificer Divine,/ Whose hand contains the earth and sky,/ Vouchsafed, as in his ark, to lie! (Venantius Fortunatus). Radiant and serene, she seems to stand on a threshold: on the threshold of the life she carries within her, which will span the Passion and the Resurrection, originally depicted on the facing panel of the triptych. The child taking flesh within Mary is the Son of God. By his Passion and his victory over death, he comes to seal the eternal convenant between God his Father and humankind. By his Incarnation, this redemption is made possible. The sweet contemplative face of the Virgin proclaims this promise. And is the color of her blouse not that of hope? Her silhouette, standing out in profile against a black background, arouses tender emotion. Her ample cloak underscores the rounded shape of her womb, the unmistakeable sign of her condition. The immaculate brilliance of her gown matches the luminous halo of she who welcomes the earthshaking presence of the Redeemer with profound humility. The Virgin's demeanor—her lowered eyes, lost in thought, with a hint of a smile—foreshadows the words of Luke: "*His mother kept all these things in her heart*" (Lk 2:51). But we have not yet arrived at those moments of sorrow that will pierce her heart (see Lk 2:35). Until then, let us enter with Mary into the Expectation.

How long the people of Israel had been waiting! How patient, the elect, to endure the reprimands, the remonstrations, the testing by the prophets! But how tiresome too, this spoiled child who forgets on the morrow the deeds performed for him by the Lord the day before; who listens only to his stomach and to his feet in the desert when his God desires to speak to his heart; who hears only false prophets when his God sends him authentic witnesses. How we resemble this fickle Israel, in our faith as in our doubts, in our heroism as in our infidelities, in our docility to the Spirit as in our formalistic worship, in our generous impulses as in our hardness of heart!

Since the fall of Adam, humanity has hoped for a Savior. Mythic at first, the promise of a redeemer became more defined over the course of the centuries, and Israel retained in its memory his heraldings, and in its heros his prefigurements. Abel, the good shepherd murdered through jealousy; Joseph, sold by his brothers; Melchizedek, priest of the Most High, who offered bread and wine in sacrifice; Isaac, bound on the wood as a holocaust; Moses the liberator and supreme lawmaker; Joshua, who led his people into the Holy Land; David, the king according to the heart of God; Solomon, the fount of wisdom; Jeremiah, through whose lips the message of the simple-hearted confounded wise men and scholars—all depict some aspect of the face of the One who is to come.

Paolo Caliari, called Veronese (1528–1588), *The Sacrifice of Isaac*, (c. 1586), oil on canvas, 50.8 x 37.4 in.

Is this some "holy slaughter"? A crime legitimized by God himself? No! The sacrifice of Isaac by his father Abraham is a symbol of the absolute confidence of the believer in the Word of God—a foreshadowing of Christ's sacrifice on the cross and the bloodless sacrifice of the Eucharist. What's more, the fourth verse of the biblical story (Gn 22:4) speaks of a divine revelation on the third day…. Abraham obeyed the Lord's command without hesitation and thus finds himself at the designated site. The drama mounts and unfolds in an instant. Alone, without a cry, his eyes lowered, unaware of any divine intervention, Isaac offers himself, a willing and resigned martyr. Abraham is stopped in the act by the angel: "*Do not lay your hand on the boy,*" says the messenger. "*Do not do the least thing to him. I know now how devoted your are to God, since you did not withhold from me your own beloved son*" (Gn 22:12). In the biblical text, Abraham is not stopped by the angel's arm, but by his words. The artist's staging of the scene heightens the dramatic effect. What skill in the plunge of this angel whose shadow veils the patriarch's face while at the same time bearing with him the source of light! The brilliance and the fluttering folds of his gilded cloak reflect the flight of a seraph while contrasting with the classical austerity of the altar. Hidden in the foliage, a lamb observes the scene. It is he who will be offered in sacrifice, until the Son of Man, Isaac in his full manifestation, the Son of the Father, accomplishes the ultimate sacrifice of his life on the cross of the definitive covenant.

Even animals and objects revealed some features of the Savior to come: the tree of life, Noah's ark, the paschal lamb, manna, the ark of the covenant, etc., all are symbolic illustrations, prefigurements of a life story. Thus, the inspired portrait of the Anointed One became more and more precisely defined, that everyone might recognize him at the fulfillment of the ages. He will be a son of man, born of a young woman (Is 7:14), the same who will strike the head of the serpent (Gn 3:15); he will be of the people of Abraham, Isaac, and Jacob. Of the house of David, he will be born in Bethlehem (Mi 5:1); he will take the royal scepter and the mace of authority in the heart of the tribe of Judah (Gn 49:10); just and victorious, he will make himself lowly, to triumph seated upon the foal of a donkey (Zec 9:9).

And now history itself becomes preparatory of the event of salvation: the liberation from slavery in Egypt and the return from captivity in Babylon enter into human destiny like metaphorical heralds of the sovereign freedom with which the Messiah was to bless humanity held captive to sin, just as the destruction of Carthage augured the definitive defeat of the empire of evil.

While Jerusalem, the Holy City, already gave glimpses of the coming splendor of the Christian Church, the Jews dispersed and founded communities throughout the inhabited world, making known to the pagans the name and the glory of the God of Abraham, Isaac, and Jacob. Translated into Greek, the most widely used language in the world at the time, the Law and the Prophets, the light of Israel, began to become the light of the world. Even profane philosophers began preparing the human race for knowledge of the truth, providing in advance well-grounded arguments for those who, in the name of the living and true God, would awaken the pagan world from its ignorance.

And thus it was that the coming prepared for more than four thousand years, the mystery foretold by Isaiah, Jeremiah, Micah, Zechariah, Daniel, and the other prophets, the mystery passed on in vigil gatherings, meditated in the synagogues, preserved in exile, the mystery longed for by so many hearts since the dawn of time was to become a reality fulfilled within human history.

Just as the eating of the fruit of the tree of the knowledge of good and evil brought death into the garden of Eden, salvation was to come through the tree of life, rooted in the lineage of Jesse and fulfilled in Mary, wife of Joseph son of David. The journey traveled by Israel can be traced in its branches with its kings and its prophets. The Redeemer will be a son of man, from a real family, with a real genealogy. He will take a name, that of his tribe, that name which defines us, that identifies us, that connects us to a land, a kinship, a history, our history. The Savior of the world will be true man, one of us.

Michelangelo Buonarroti (1475–1564), *David* (1501–1504), detail, marble sculpture, 161 in.

Michelangelo evokes the biblical episode of David, the young shepherd chosen by Samuel to be king of Israel, pitted against Goliath. His face, portrayed in classical style and framed by abundant curls, takes its inspiration from the biblical text: *"He was youthful, and ruddy, and handsome in appearance"* (1 Sm 17:42). This is not the face of a victorious warrior, nor that of a powerful king: it is one whose trust is in God, who alone grants victory. The odds are stacked against David, facing the giant Goliath. It is surely a mixed feeling of fear and confidence that furrows his brow. His piercing stare, too, betrays contained turmoil. The story of David takes on a prophetic dimension. The hope of the people of Israel who await a new David is embodied in Jesus, the "Son of David" sent by God. The coming of Christ is necessary, that the promises made to David may be fully accomplished.

VIRGO · DEI · GENITRIX · VIRGA · EST · FLOS · FILIVS · EIVS

EGREDIETVR · VIRGA · DE · RADICE · VESSE · YSAIE · XIC

ANO · A · PARTV · VRGNIS · SALVTIFERO · M · V · PRIMO
PRESIDENTE · IN · LOCO · ISTO · BNDO · PRE · F · I · W
HANS · HOLBAIN · DE · AVGVSTA · ME · PINXIT

VIRGO·DEIFERA·FLORID·PDICATOR· ORDIS·SIGVLARIS·PATRONA·

HENRICVS·SVSE·HOROIO
CII·ET·OMES·APIECE·MIESTO·DVT

ANTHONINARG·
HIEPS·FLERENTINVS·
SVMISTA·EGREGIVS·

ENHABITVS·ORDIS·TVI

VINCENCVS·BELACENS
SPECLATOR·OMIS·
MATRIE·SCIBILIS·

M·MAGR·REGNALDS·PRIECBVS·SCI·DNIC
ABLIT·QVI·ILIT·PER·VIRGIAM·MARIAM·CRAT·
HABIT·ORDINISAR·CONV·OVSERT

PETRVS·DE·PALVDE·PATRIACHA·IHEROSO
ET·PFET·THEOLOG·ET·PRI·THOMISTA·ROMA

RAIMVDVS·CATHOISTA·PRCELLETISSIM?
DECRETALIVM·COLECTER

HVGO·CARDINALIS·POSTIL
LATOR·BIBLIE·PRIMVS·

NICLAVS·
PAPA·BENE

PETRVS·DE·THARENTASIA·
PAPA·INHOCENCIVS·V·

ARAS·AQVINAS·
THEOLOGORVM·
S·PETRVS·DEMEDI
OLANO·MARTIR·IX
DOCTOR·ET·VIRGO·

ALBERTVS·MAGNVS·RATISPO
EPS·DOCTOR·VNIVERSAL

S·VICENCVS·DONO·LIGVAR
PREDICATOR·GRACIOSVS·

S·
INIS·
FVDAT

MICVS·OR
CATOR
PRIMVS

ORDINEM·PREDICATIVM·PRO·SALVT·ECCLESIE·TOTIVS·
ALMA·DEI·PARENS·A·FILO·SALVATORE·GRACIOSE·
IMPETRAVIT·ANNO·SALVTIS·NOSTRE·M·CCXIIII·

O NIMIS FELIX

O more than blessed, merit high
attaining, pure as the snow-drift,
innocent of evil, child of the desert,
mightiest of martyrs,
greatest of prophets.

O may the virtue of thine intercession,
all stony hardness from our hearts
expelling, smooth the rough places,
and the crooked straighten
here in the desert.

Thus may our gracious Maker and
Redeemer, seeking a station for his
hallowed footsteps, find,
when he cometh, temples undefilèd,
meet to receive him.

Now as the angels celebrate thy praises,
Godhead essential, Trinity coequal;
spare thy redeemed ones, as they bow
before thee, pardon imploring.
Amen.

O nimis felix meritíque
celsi, nésciens labem
nívei pudóris, præpotens
martyr eremíque cultor,
máxime vatum.

Nunc potens nostri méritis
opímis péctoris duros
lápides repélle, ásperum
planans iter, et refléxos
dírige calles.

Ut pius mundi sator et
redémptor, méntibus pulsa
mácula polítis, rite dignétur
véniens sacrátos pónere
gressus.

Láudibus cives célebrant
supérni te, Deus simplex
paritérque trine; súpplices
ac nos véniam precámur:
parce redémptis. Amen.

THE LAST PROPHET: JOHN THE BAPTIST

*The One who is coming after me
is greater than I.*

Elizabeth and Zechariah, the parents of John the Baptist, were old and barren. They were the image of humanity which, afflicted by its age-old addiction to sin, was unable to bear any holy fruit. As with the previous miraculous births of Isaac, Samson, and Samuel, that of John prepared hardened hearts to understand that nothing is impossible for God, and to accept that it is precisely where sin once abounded that grace would overflow (Rom 5:20). We see how, already by his coming into the world, John the Precursor was preparing the way of the Lord in hearts and minds. He was preparing the people of God to listen for the unutterable, which would soon be proclaimed to them. Indeed, not only in Israel had the womb of humanity, though old and barren, produced in John the Baptist a holy fruit, but, regenerated by an amazing grace, this womb would again become more fertile than the youthful Eve, younger than sin, to bring forth into the world the holy uncreated One.

Thus, according to his vocation, John the Baptist prepared hearts to welcome the Lord, for *the kingdom of God is near* (cf. Mt 3:2). Yes, the reign of love is very near; but the reign of justice is following quickly on its heels, and John warns us that *the axe is laid to the roots of the trees, so that any tree which fails to produce good fruit will be cut down and thrown on the fire* (Lk 3:9). And he exhorts us, whose souls, grown old in our habits of sin, have become barren: *"Produce good fruits as evidence of your repentance"* (cf. Lk 3:8). Today, when we are sinners, not through weakness as in the days of the self-proclaimed righteous of Israel, but through design, sinners in the name of great principles, even in the name of the rights of man—the rights of man without God!—let us be jolted by the word of John the Baptist, just as John the Baptist himself in his mother's womb was jolted when, upon hearing Mary's greeting, he experienced the close proximity of the Savior (Lk 1:41).

Anton Raphaël Mengs (1728–1779), *Saint John the Baptist Preaching in the Desert* (1765), oil on canvas, 81.9 x 60.2 in.

Through the genius of Mengs, we can hear the voice of the prophet crying out in the desert: *Prepare a way for the Lord, make his paths straight!* (Mk 1:3). No mild-mannered, impersonal speeches from this man's lips, but rather a sharp, direct rebuke, a call to radical conversion—a call that is embodied in the fiery look of this man, his vigorous body coiled and ready to spring. Impetuosity and conviction can be read in this face and in these outstretched hands that catch the shimmer of golden light. We see a snapshot before us. The Precursor has just leaned his cross-shaped staff against a withered tree trunk, a reference to his ascetic life. His traditional garb of an animal pelt is partially hidden under the voluminous folds of a scarlet mantle, foreshadowing the blood that will flow at the tragic moment of his martyrdom. The man of the desert, the man of absolutes, John the Baptist is uncompromising. The call he issued in the Judean desert is renewed in these days, as we prepare for the new coming of the Lord in our hearts.

INCLITOS CHRISTI

Singing, we laurel Christ's heroic servants, rightly renowned for faith and deeds bright shining, for on this feast day, earth unites with heaven, chanting their praises.

They lived on earth so meek and pure and humble, building up lifetimes innocent of evil, until their spirits flew from earth in freedom, to starry heaven.

Now from the heav'ns they joy to help the lowly, wiping the tears of all who mourn in sadness, mending the varied wounds of mind and body, healing our illness.

Let praise resound for these, God's kindly servants, thanks let us give these ever-ready helpers who come to aid us with their loving power in all our troubles.

To God alone be dignity and power, praise in the highest, honor everlasting, who governs all things, in the earth and heavens, in peaceful order. Amen.

Inclitos Christi fámulos canámus, quos, fide claros nitidísque gestis, hac die tellus sociáta cælo láudibus ornat.

Quippe qui mites, húmiles, pudíci, nésciam culpæ coluére vitam, donec e terris ánimus volávit liber ad astra.

Inde iam gaudent míseris adésse, fléntium tergunt lácrimas, medéntur méntium plagis, vitiáta reddunt membra salúti.

Nostra laus ergo résonet benígnis his Dei servis referátque grates, qui pia pergant ope nos iuváre rebus in arctis.

Sit Deo soli decus et potéstas, laus in excélsis, honor ac perénnis, qui suis totum móderans gubérnat légibus orbem. Amen.

THE MARRIAGE
OF JOSEPH AND MARY

All you who love Jerusalem, rejoice with her for ever.

The Jews of Judea said that nothing good could come out of Galilee (cf. Jn 1:46). Yet it was in this cosmopolitan province that around the year AD 5 Joseph, a carpenter of Nazareth, was preparing to celebrate his marriage to a young woman named Mary. Joseph was a Jew of the tribe of Judah and a descendant of King David. He was a true son of Israel, in his genealogy as in his heart. He may have been about twenty-five years old. Mary, his betrothed, was a very young maiden who was probably between thirteen and sixteen. Schooled in the Psalms, the Law, and the Prophets, she found in them the words of her thoughts and the inspiration of her spontaneous prayer.

Since the promises had been exchanged in a private ceremony in the presence of their two families, Joseph and Mary were considered definitively married. It would have taken the due process of an act of repudiation for Joseph to withdraw. In any case, the two espoused were not living together, and custom dictated that their union not be consummated until Joseph received his bride under his roof, following the wedding feast that would take place about one year after the exchange of promises.

While the wedding preparations were well under way, Mary was turning over in her heart an event that was beyond her: for three months now, in accordance with the pronouncement of an angel who had appeared to her, she was pregnant. Who would comprehend her secret? Not that it was unspeakable; it was inexpressible. And so, at night, like all mothers the world over, Mary would place her hands on her belly until she could feel the fruit of her womb quickening under her palms. And she spoke to him, endlessly repeating to him the words the angel had spoken to her on behalf of the Lord: *"Listen! You are to conceive and bear a son.... The Holy Spirit will come upon you.... the child will be holy and will be called Son of God* (Lk 1:31, 35). For nothing will be impossible for God.... The angel proclaimed it to me, and now it is done: you are there, my Child. You are there: peace and joy fill my heart. You are there and my joy is complete; I am the happiest among women and my spirit exults in God my Savior."

But Mary's thoughts were also with Joseph, her sweet spouse. Having given her promise to bring him happiness, she was yet about to make him undergo the worst of sufferings. How would he bear what he could only understand as a betrayal? How would she herself bear to soon read that horrible certitude in her beloved's eyes? *"Do not be afraid"*, the angel of the Lord had said to her (Lk 1:30). And so, with the invincible confidence that came from her innate innocence, Mary placed her fate in the hands of God: *"I am the handmaid of the Lord, let what you have said be done to me"* (Lk 1:38).

Domenikos Theotokopoulos, called **El Greco** (1541–1614), *The Marriage of the Virgin* (1610), oil on canvas, 43.3 x 32.7 in.

The marriage of the Virgin and Joseph is found in the "apocryphal Gospels" and in the *Golden Legend* of Jacobus de Voragine. Breaking with iconographic tradition, the artist abandons the pyramidal composition and the frieze dear to artists of the Renaissance. Architectural elements are replaced by the voluptuous folds of a large wall hanging that recalls the veil of the Temple. In this static liturgy, a circle of majestic figures opens out toward the viewer, allowing us to admire the gesture of the high priest joining the hands of Mary and Joseph. Guided by the perspective of the floor tiles, our gaze then moves from this focal point to linger over the textures of the ample robes: the silky sky-blue sheen of the Virgin's mantle, the golden yellow folds of Joseph's cloak, not to mention the shimmering satin vestment of the celebrant. The virtuosity of El Greco clothes each actor here with the divine Presence. In their stature, their dignity, their nobility, they are consecrated. By entering Jesus into the legitimate descendance of Joseph, this union makes possible the coming of the Messiah, the fulfillment of Isaiah's prophecy. Only the white-bearded man looks out toward us, a mute witness inviting us to welcome, along with this newlywed couple, the will of God in our lives.

TE IOSEPH CELEBRENT

Joseph! to thee by hosts on high
and choirs of Christians,
laud be paid! Saintly of life,
by purest tie joined unto her,
the glorious Maid.

When thou didst doubt thy wife's
repute, and mark her great with
motherhood, the angel taught thee that
her fruit came from the Holy Ghost
of God.

Spare us, O Trinity most high!
Grant that, with Joseph, we may gain
thy starry realm, and ceaselessly
there raise to thee our thankful
strain. Amen.

Te, Ioseph, célebrent
ágmina cælitum, te cuncti
résonent Christíadum chori,
qui, clarus méritis, iunctus
es ínclitæ casto fœdere Vírgini.

Almo cum túmidam gérmine
cóniugem admírans, dúbio
tángeris ánxius, afflátu súperi
Fláminis ángelus concéptum
púerum docet.

Nobis, summa Trias, parce
precántibus; da Ioseph méritis
sídera scándere, ut tandem
líceat nos tibi pérpetim gratum
prómere cánticum. Amen.

28

THE DREAM OF JOSEPH

The just man shall blossom like the lily, alleluia.
He shall flourish for ever in the courts of our God, alleluia.

One day, what was bound to happen happened: Joseph learned that his beloved wife was pregnant, certainly by someone other than himself, since he had scrupulously respected the customs. How did Mary respond to his demands for an explanation? Her response undoubtedly bore the irresistible hallmarks of such truth that Joseph's suspicions were allayed.

Joseph knew Mary like a book, by heart: that she could have lied while swearing to him before God that she had not known any man was beyond the realm of possibility. And yet his beloved was well and truly pregnant! Despite the irrefutable fact, Joseph resisted an incessant undertow of doubts through personal conviction: with the soul of a pious man, just and righteous, he had recognized in Mary's soul an Edenic innocence. What else could he do but allow Mary to leave to fulfill her mysterious destiny? Rather than publicly denouncing her, which would have been tantamount to handing her over for stoning, he resolved, against all probability, to credit this mystery. He would thus repudiate Mary, but quietly and with honor.

However, one morning as Joseph awoke, his entire being was again thrown into turmoil through one of those dreams that make more of an impression on the soul than the most tangible reality. An angel had appeared to him, sent by the Lord: *"Joseph son of David, do not be afraid to take Mary home as your wife, because she has conceived what is in her by the Holy Spirit. She will give birth to a son and you must name him Jesus"* (Mt 1:20-21). Called upon to name the child according to Jewish tradition, Joseph knew that he was indisputably the father; not an adoptive father, but rather a father adopted by his own child—his God!—from the moment of his conception as true man in the womb of Mary.

From that day, Joseph had the sure awareness that the mysterious fruit his beloved spouse was carrying was blessed, and that his marriage was not destroyed but rather transcended by this blessing. In the strength of this conviction, joined with the hope of Israel within him, Joseph welcomed his wife Mary into their conjugal home. Thus, through the grace of their marriage, the *Son of the Most High* would be born a true *son of David* (cf. Mt 1:1).

The Dream of Joseph (1175), capital, cloister of the monastery of San Juan de la Peña, Spain.

Throughout salvation history, God has used different means to reveal himself and make his thoughts known. The dream is one of them. We are witnesses to this singular tête-à-tête, so candidly and amiably expressed by the Romanesque sculptor. Joseph receives the visit of the angel, who addresses him through the medium of a dream. But this message takes a concrete, physical form. The heavenly messenger places his hand on the sleeping man's chest. He touches him to the depths of his heart, as his wing brushes Joseph's feet, hidden under the elegant folds of a blanket. Thus it is with his whole being that Joseph will obey the voice of the Spirit speaking through this dream, that he will respond, through love of God and love of Mary, to the desire to see the plans of the Lord fulfilled.

The two figures are perfectly integrated within the confined surface of a capital, the decorative part at the top of a column. The angel leans with perfect naturalness on the thick cushion, as though to buffer his precipitous arrival. We find this spontaneity magnified by the incomparable style of the eleventh century. The wide-open eyes of the angel, like two protruding marbles, stare at the sleeper's serene face, dominated by his almond-shaped closed eyes. Thus, happily far from the commonplace dream interpretations of fortune-tellers or even psychoanalysts, art allows the transcription of the mystery of divine revelation communicated by the Holy Spirit.

VERBUM SALUTIS OMNIUM

The Savior of all men, the Word,
who from the Father's mouth
proceeds, within your womb, O Virgin
blest, we humbly beg you to receive.

The Spirit overshadows you,
his fruitful work has now begun,
that you might bring forth Christ
the Lord, the Father's coeternal Son.

Behold the sacred temple's gate,
remaining sealed for years unknown;
its blessed threshold fastened tight
would open for the Prince alone.

Of old the prophets held his pledge;
before the dawn he had his birth;
now Gabriel proclaims to you:
the Lord descends unto the earth.

Verbum salútis ómnium,
Patris ab ore pródiens,
Virgo beáta, súscipe casto,
María, víscere.

Te nunc illústrat cælitus
umbra fecúndi Spiritus,
gestes ut Christum Dóminum,
æquálem Patri Fílium.

Hæc est sacráti iánua
templi seráta iúgiter,
soli suprémo Príncipi
pandens beáta límina.

Olim promíssus vátibus,
natus ante lucíferum,
quem Gabriél annúntiat,
terris descéndit Dominus.

THE JOURNEY FROM
NAZARETH
TO BETHLEHEM

*Joseph left Nazareth and set out for the town of David
called Bethlehem to register with Mary.*

A few months after Joseph had received Mary into his home, when her pregnancy was reaching its term, he was obliged to undertake a journey to Bethlehem, the town of his ancestors, in compliance with the decree of the Roman emperor. For a great census had been ordered of all the inhabitants of the empire, each summoned to go to be enrolled in his native town. Historical research confirms that such a census did take place, probably in the year 6 or 7 BC. It also attests that it was the responsibility of the "master of the house" to declare all members of his family, as well as any guests, employees, or slaves, and, if possible, to go and make the declaration in his home district. In these circumstances, it might have been prudent for Joseph to entrust the young Mary to the care of their family. But he could not resign himself to this, unwilling to leave his beloved wife behind at this critical time, when she might yet be the object of reproof to some still suspicious of her having conceived, before custom deemed it entirely proper. Whatever the case, the wise Joseph considered there no sufficient cause to delegate his blessed ministry as protector of the Mother of God and of the divine Child. At that time, the ninety-mile journey was not considered too adventurous. It was the same as the pilgrimage to Jerusalem that Joseph made every year, which was only a four-to-five day trip. In such cases, one normally joined very well-organized caravans to ensure that the journey was safe, relatively comfortable, and socially enriching. Joseph probably mounted Mary and a

few supplies on the donkey he normally used to deliver his carpentry work…
and thus set off to inscribe into the History of the World the greatest news
ever told by God: *"A Savior is born to you!"* (cf. Lk 2:11).

The Enrollment in Bethlehem before Governor Quirinius (1407–1413),
fresco, Monastery of Kalenic, Serbia.

Two specific names are mentioned in the Gospel of Luke: *"Now at this time Caesar Augustus issued
a decree for a census of the whole world to be taken. This census—the first—took place while Quirinius was
governor of Syria, and everyone went to his own town to be registered"* (Lk 2:1-3). If we know the famous
emperor, the same cannot be said for this administrator, a seasoned general who, despite his
mention here, remains unknown to many of us. The inspiration of this artist who worked on
the remarkable fresco cycle for the Serbian monastery of Kalenic puts a face to the name for
us. In conjunction with the Scriptures, it helps us to concretely grasp his role. With a touching
freshness, it is the governor himself who directs the census. Is this to indicate that this man and
woman who have reported to Bethlehem are worthy of his rank, indeed outrank him, given the
importance of the mission that is theirs? The couple is presented in the courtyard of a palace,
beneath the shade of a majestically unfurled velarium. Similar prestige is added through the figure
of Quirinius, enthroned with guards by his side, while a functionary enrolls the names of Joseph
and Mary on a scroll of parchment. Even before his birth, Jesus inscribes himself in human history. Let us rejoice, for we are part of the people of God, a people too numerous to count and of
which the Lord knows every member to the depths of their innermost being!

MAGNIS PROPHETÆ
VOCIBUS

The prophets with how great a voice
told the redemption of our race!
Those first to hail him might rejoice,
the Christ who saves us by his grace.

Of old the prior advent was
no punishment. A gift God gave
to cleanse our ancient wound, because
by this might Christ the lost souls save.

To us now a second is made known;
Christ at the earthly gate doth call,
come to give saints their promised
crown, and spread the realm celestial.

Now light eternal forth is sent,
now too a saving star doth shine,
a beacon in the firmament
that calls us toward the Law divine.

You, Christ, oh you alone we seek
to see, who are yourself the Light,
that endless may be Praise's song,
eternal too the blessed sight. Amen.

Magnis prophétæ vócibus
veníre Christum núntiant,
lætæ salútis prævia,
qua nos redémit, grátia.

Advéntus hic primus fuit,
puníre quo non sæculum
venit, sed ulcus térgere,
salvándo quod períerat.

At nos secúndus præmonet
adésse Christum iánuis,
sanctis corónas réddere
cælíque regna pándere.

Ætérna lux promíttitur
sidúsque salvans prómitur;
iam nos iubar præfúlgidum
ad ius vocat cæléstium.

Te, Christe, solum quærimus
vidére, sicut es Deus,
ut perpes haec sit vísio
perénne laudis cánticum. Amen.

THE ARRIVAL
IN BETHLEHEM

*But you Bethlehem-Ephrathah, too small to be among the clans of
Judah, from you shall come forth for me one who is to be ruler
in Israel.*

The influx of travelers come to Bethlehem to be enrolled in the census register meant the only place left to accomodate Joseph and Mary was a stable. What a worthy shelter for he who would later say of himself: *"Foxes have dens and birds of the sky have nests, but the Son of Man has nowhere to rest his head"* (Lk 9:58). Since his parents made a manger his cradle, from the moment of his birth in the world, God-with-us had nowhere to lay his head....

And so Jesus was born, poor among the poor, but because of his royal genealogy, he was born in Bethlehem. For he was of the tribe of Judah (cf. Heb 8:8) and the son of David. In order to fulfill Scripture, it was necessary that the child of the promise should have as ancestors all the kings of Judah descended from David. However, the decay which, in the end, overcomes all human grandeur was such that Joseph's august lineage was not manifested in the prestige of a great house, but rather in the lowliness of a modest family of craftsmen. Right from the start, it had to be clearly evident that Jesus' royalty was of a different nature and of a different significance than that transmitted by blood. From the moment of Jesus' birth, it was strikingly apparent that it is the prerogative of divine omnipotence to manifest itself right within the heart of human frailty. And thus, from the pitiful manger where he lay bound in swaddling clothes, totally powerless to act, the newborn Jesus has mysteriously *shown the strength of his arm, he has scattered the proud in their conceit. He has cast down the mighty from their thrones, and has lifted up the lowly* (cf. Lk 1:52).

Luc-Olivier Merson (1846–1920), *The Arrival in Bethlehem* (1897), oil on canvas, 31.9 x 21.3 in.

In this painting, designed like an opera set, drama rivals with pathos. In the foreground, on the point of exhaustion, Mary expresses forlorn resignation through the tightly closed eyes and ashen face worthy of a tragic actress. Joseph is once again turned down by an innkeeper who doesn't even deign to open her door. "Go somewhere else," she seems to shout at the traveler who knows not where to turn. They must hurry; night is falling and stray dogs are on the prowl. Why—as so often in the history of art—has the painter depicted a rather elderly Joseph? He was no doubt inspired by an episode in the *Protoevangelium of James*, which quotes Joseph as saying, "I am an old man, and she is a young girl. I am afraid lest I become a laughing-stock to the sons of Israel." This text recounts that Mary, feeling that the baby was on the way, asked to dismount from the donkey. To which Joseph responded, "Whither shall I lead you, and cover your disgrace? For the place is a desert." But *"there was no room for them at the inn"* (Lk 2:7). This exclusion would later be linked by commentators to Saint John's affirmation: *"He came to his own domain, and his own people did not accept him"* (Jn 1:11). Merson's "romantic" vision, amplified by a heritage of certain picturesque traditions, makes us alive to a fundamental question: "Can God truly enter into my life unless I open the door of my soul to him?"

THE NATIVITY

Marvelous is the mystery proclaimed today:
man's nature is made new as God becomes man; he remains
what he was and becomes what he was not.
Yet each nature stays distinct and for ever undivided.

In 1952, *Life Magazine* commissioned this stained glass for the Christmas celebrations at Rockefeller Center in New York. The great light of the star shines over a landscape of organic shapes. Earth and sky interlink; stars seem to leave their imprint on the green grass as they intermingle with plants and flowers. This Christmas night draws the old world from its torpor, dazzling it with this incomparable long-desired presence.

Matisse's artistic explorations, which reflect his attachment to form and chromatics, is characterized here by the sculptural dimension of the contours of the glass panes, as well as the luminosity of each large patch of color. Here color evokes movement, and the shapes, lush vegetation. The result is particularly effective, the source of vivacity and dynamism. A transcription of ineffable joy, this stained glass window can be likened to the paper cut-outs Matisse created when illness prevented him from painting. As the artist himself wrote, he considered stained glass "like a musical score played by an orchestra." Each color is a tone in a veritable celebration of joy, from a man over eighty years old.

T he *Logos* became flesh *and made his dwelling among us* (cf. Jn 1:14). From the creation of the human race, man and woman, in the image and likeness of God, until Christmas night—by way of the Fall, the patriarchs, the prophets, and the kings of Israel—the Nativity of the Lord takes its place within our earthly history. And yet, the Prologue of the fourth Gospel invites us to lift ourselves up, to try to contemplate this event from a heavenly point of view.

In the beginning was the Word, the *Logos*. Before he was conceived in the womb of the Virgin Mary, Christ was. Even before the beginning of all things, Christ was. He was the One who is. He was in the beginning, but he himself did not have a beginning. No one made him, no one created him: *he was*. And what was he? He was the Word, the *Logos*, meaning that he was the infinite thought within God, the eternal design, the personified and active word.

At the creation of the world, *Through him all things came to be, not one thing had its being but through him. All that came to be had life in him* (Jn 1:3-4a).

Jean-Charles-Nicaise Perrin (1754–1831), *The Nativity* (1784), oil on canvas, Church of Saint Louis-en-l'Île, Paris

"All that came to be had life in him and that life was the light of men, a light that shines in the dark, a light that darkness could not overpower" (Jn 1:4-5). These words of John the Evangelist take on particuliar resonance as we contemplate this canvas. The Child Jesus is the unique source of light, making the figures of Mary and Joseph surge out of the darkness. We are reminded that, by coming into the world, the Son of God, "Light born of light," brings creation out of the shadows into which it had been plunged through sin. In this holy night, *"The Word was the true light that enlightens all men"* (Jn 1:9). This radiating light lends the scene all its sacred character, heightened by the otherwordly halo—a pale reflection of the divine light—of the herald angel addressing the shepherds in the background. The nativity of Christ is a mystery much greater than the birth of the Child Jesus: it is the coming into the world of he who comes to transform all, just as the light in this canvas caresses, reveals, and transforms the colors and the faces of the protagonists.

The voluminous folds of the clothing, the handling of the skin tones and materials, these attest to the painter's affinity to the Flemish tradition. The sobriety of the composition and the interiority of the expressions focus on the essential. When we confess that the Child in the manger is the Son of God, we affirm that the God who was born in our human flesh gives us birth into his divine life.

Fritz von Uhde (1848–1911), *Holy Night* (1888–1889), triptych, oil on canvas, 52.8 x 84.6 in. Through the traditional format of this canvas, the artist vies with the great triptychs of the past, and seeks to go beyond them. Mary has just given birth to the Child. Now *in the country-side close by there were shepherds who lived in the fields and took it in turns to watch their flocks during the night* (Lk 2:8). As often happens in the history of art, the assocation of several moments in the Nativity story allows the artist to fuse the narrative into the particular space that is the triptych. On the left, emerging from the gloom of a forest, their lanterns underscoring the surrounding darkness, contemporary workers replace the traditional shepherds, their bodies bent and faces lined by their labor (continued on page 53).

In the beginning, the *Logos was in God* (Jn 1:1b). He had his being in God. He was in God a Person. He was a a divine Person. He *was God* (Jn 1:1c). Was he the one God? Yes, he was. Was he the only God? Yes, he was. Was he the only divine Person in God? No, for this God who was in the beginning and though whom all things came to be, *we saw his glory, the glory that is his as the only Son of the Father* (Jn 1:14). The *Logos* was *the only begotten Son, who is in the bosom of the Father* (cf. Jn 1:18). Thus, at the beginning was the living and true God: the Father and the Son in the communion of the Holy Spirit.

Before time, there was nothing in the *Logos* that had been made. But when time came to be, he who was begotten, not made, he who was God born of God and Light born of Light, he who always was and will be for ever, he was made. And what was he made? He was made man. He was God of eternity; he was made flesh within time… and for all time!

The divine *Logos, the true light that enlightens all men* (Jn 1:9) came to be born and dwell among us like one of us; but, even more, he was one of us. And, for all those who recognize him and believe in his name, *he gave power to become children of God* (Jn 1:12). To recognize him means to recognize him for what he is: the true and living God. To believe in his name means to believe that he is the only Son who became man, that all men might be adopted children of God by the Father. To believe in the name of Jesus Christ means to believe that our Lord and God, through his human Nativity, became the firstborn of a multitude of brothers, sons of God.

Believe in the love God has had for us (cf. 1 Jn 4:16), a love in which God gives us not only all he has, but all he is as well. Then the Psalmist will rightly proclaim these words of God upon our heads: *I declare: "You are gods, offspring of the Most High all of you"* (cf. Ps 81:6). *And the* Logos *became flesh and made his dwelling among us* (Jn 1:14a). Henceforth we have the power to become children of God. Of course, Jesus Christ alone is *full of grace and truth* (Jn 1:14), but it is for us that he has been so filled, for us who *receive from his fullness grace upon grace* (cf. Jn 1:16).

When the *Logos* became flesh, God emerged—so to speak—from his august and impenetrable mystery. The Inaccessible rendered himself adorable to our senses. The Incomparable made of man his equals. And he accomplished this wonder in a way well beyond our imagining. For, as Bossuet put it: "Being infinitely good, he is infinitely communicative, infinitely unifying, so that we must not be surprised that he should unite human nature to his divine Person. He may elevate man as much as he pleases, even to the point of being one person with him." Or, in the words of Saint Leo the Great: "By taking human nature, the Word elevates that which he takes on, without losing that which he communicates."

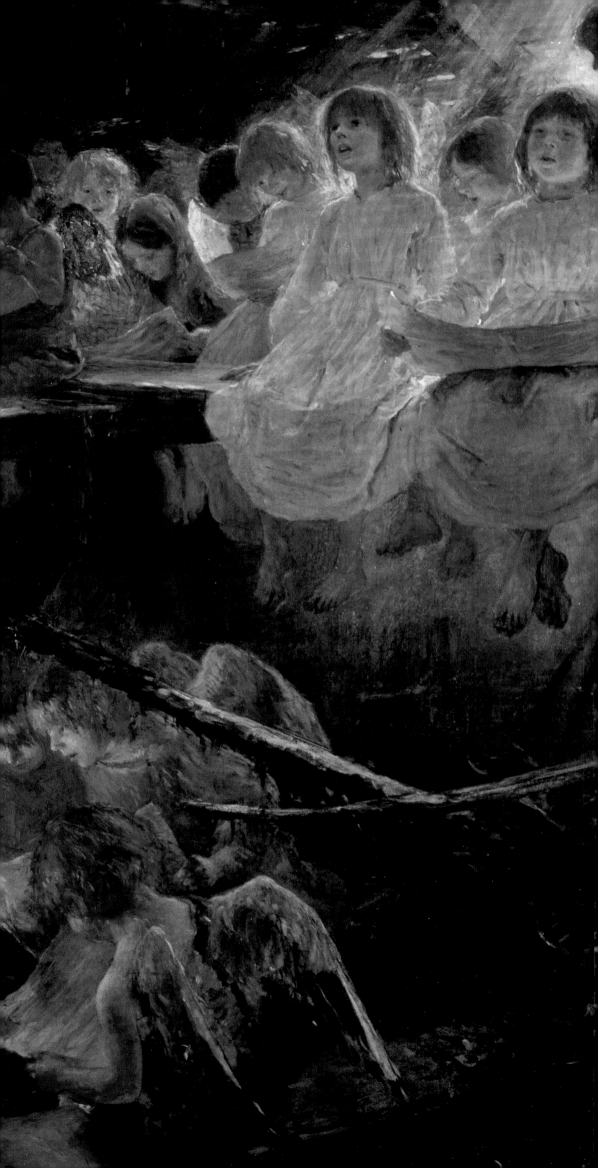

In the right-hand panel, angels form the heavenly beneficent host, singing, *"Glory to God in the highest heaven, and peace to men who enjoy his favor"* (Lk 2:14). One could never tire of contemplating the variety of features of these little children. They are seated in joyous ranks in a half-ruined loft traversed by beams of divine light. More or less concentrating on their sheet music, their song rings out to those come to welcome the One before whom Mary now sits in adoration on the edge of a crude mattress. Joseph has withdrawn to the stairs, lost in contemplation of infinity—the vanishing point of the impressive lines of perspective that extend the length of this poor hovel. As we share in Joseph's deep meditation, let us admire just a few of the many artistic gems, such as the warm light of the lantern illuminating both Mother and Child, as well as the three angels bent over their sheet music....

In the beginning, man wished to become Godlike by eating of the fruit of the tree of the knowledge of good and evil. Ever since then, his pride has never ceased pushing him to desire to become a little god through the conquest of sham attributes of divine sovereignty: might, power, riches, glory. Although, while he would make himself god out of pride, here is God who makes himself man out of love. Yes, it was truly to enable us to become God that God made himself man! Will the effect of the Incarnation be to satisfy our pride, aroused by the jealousy of the devil? Certainly not! For the Child God in the manger revealed to us that pride completely deceives us: by giving us a radically false idea of God, it leads to our perdition by making us, in a way, jealous of a God who does not exist, but is the product of our own concupiscence. It is precisely for this reason that, to communicate himself to us, to open us to what God truly is, the unbegotten Word divests himself of his sovereign majesty and infinite might. We wish to become like gods? Let us become like Jesus Christ! Let us be weak, humble, poor, pure of heart, merciful, just. Let us love to the point of offering the greatest proof of love: our life for those whom we love. In a word, if we wish to become God, let us be saints. For then we shall be true children of our heavenly Father, who is holy. And we shall be true brothers and sisters of the Son of the true God, who is just born true man.

THE NAMES
OF THE CHILD-GOD

The virgin shall be with child and bear a son, and they shall
name him Emmanuel, which means "God is with us."

The Virgin is alone in adoration before her Child lying directly on the ground. While a seraph hurries to announce the birth of the Messiah to a shepherd kneeling on a hilltop, the dove of the Holy Spirit bears witness—as does the gilded halo surrounding Jesus—to the divinity of the newborn Child. Without fanfare, we are quietly entered into the intimate world of Mary.

Like many of his successors, the painter drew inspiration from the *Revelations* of Saint Bridget of Sweden: "Her most beautiful hair—as if of gold—cascaded over her shoulders…. I saw that glorious infant lying on the earth, naked and glowing in greatest purity…. When therefore the Virgin felt that she had now given birth, at once, having bowed her head and joined her hands, with great dignity and reverence she adored the boy and said to him: 'Welcome, my God, my Lord, and my son!'" (Bk 6, ch. 21, 67-68).

At this moment, Mary has not yet laid the child in the manger; the donkey and the ox await him in the back of this stable located in an austere, arid, bleak landscape. This personal encounter allows the artist to present us with the human, accessible, and comforting nature of Mary *Theotokos*, in all her unequalled maternal tenderness. With her youthful face lost in meditation and framed in long golden-brown hair; her hands placidly crossed over her breast as if to assist her humble prayerfulness, in purity and in peace of heart; her ample yet sober mantle whose hem just brushes the brilliant halo—all make of this sweet young woman an invitation to the contemplation of the *Sun of Justice* (Mal 3:20).

T he name of the Child-God was officially given to him in the ceremony of the circumcision (cf. Lk 2:21) by his father, Joseph, according to the instruction he received in a dream from the angel of the Lord (cf. Mt 1:21). And this name was "Jesus." In Hebrew, *Yeshua* means "savior." It is a diminutive, relatively common at the time, for *Yehoshua*, meaning "God saves." And Jesus really is our Savior: he saves us from the power of evil by taking our sins upon himself and by showing us the way to holiness, that we might commit them no more. So doing, he leads us to eternal life, where evil and death are definitively conquered. Following this stunning victory won for all mankind at the price of his life, *"all beings in the heavens, on earth and in the underworld, should bend the knee at the name of Jesus"* (Phil 2:10). Jesus is our Savior; we are saved. Jesus is the victor; victory is ours.

In the Bible, our Savior, Jesus, is referred to by more than 150 other names and titles. And not one of these mystical nicknames is superfluous, so difficult is it for human expression to fully reflect the qualities and charisms of Jesus. So it is that Isaiah describes him by name in terms resounding with rich variety: *"The people that walked in darkness has seen a great light; on those who live in a land of deep shadow a light has shone. For there is a child born for us, a son given to us and dominion is laid on his shoulders; and this is the name they give him: Wonder-Counselor, Mighty-God, Eternal-Father, Prince-of-Peace"* (Is 9:1, 5). As for the first Christians, they would make of the name Jesus a compound name, adding the qualifying noun "Christ," meaning "Anointed of the Lord," "Messiah."

William Blake (1757–1827), *The Night of Peace* (c. 1815), illustration 6 of "On the Morning of Christ's Nativity," ode by John Milton, watercolor and ink, 6.2 x 4.8 in.

According to the book of Deuteronomy, in the time of Moses the Lord was present in the ark of the covenant, preciously housed in the Meeting Tent, also called the Tabernacle. The poetic and ever so symbolic vision of William Blake places the newborn Word in a rickety construction outlined by the majestic unfurled wings of the two angels framing the composition. This is the new Tabernacle, which shelters the newborn Lord. The eye is drawn to the three central figures united in an expression of overwhelming love: the Child's forehead rests on that of his Mother, both lost in deep, restorative sleep. The elegant curve of a young Joseph molds the supple, flowing line of Mary's pose. These three bodies, like a sculptural pyramid, are enhanced by highlights of brilliant yellow. In the depths of the night shines a light: for the composition culminates in a female figure; rising in the sky and seated on a horse-drawn chariot, she holds aloft the star of Bethlehem. Light is incontestably at the heart of Blake's theme. He here illustrates the "night of peace," one of the verses from the ode "On the Morning of Christ's Nativity," written in the early seventeenth century by John Milton, who himself stressed the peaceful victory of Christ over the darkness.

A SOLIS ORTUS CARDINE

From east to west, from shore
to shore, let every heart awake
and sing the holy Child whom Mary
bore, the Christ, the everlasting King.

Behold, the world's Creator wears
the form and fashion of a slave;
our very flesh our Maker shares,
his fallen creature, man, to save.

He shrank not from the oxen's stall,
he lay within the manger bed,
and he whose bounty feedeth all
at Mary's breast himself was fed.

And while the angels in the sky
sang praise above the silent field,
to shepherds poor the Lord Most High,
the one great Shepherd, was revealed.

All glory for this blessèd morn
to God the Father ever be;
all praise to thee, O Virgin-born,
all praise, O Holy Ghost, to thee.
Amen.

A solis ortus cárdine
Ad úsque terræ límitem,
Christum canámus príncipem,
natum María Vírgine.

Beátus auctor sæculi
servíle corpus índuit,
ut carne carnem líberans
non pérderet quod cóndidit.

Fæno iacére pértulit,
præsépe non abhórruit,
parvóque lacte pastus est
per quem nec ales ésurit.

Gaudet chorus cæléstium
et ángeli canunt Deum,
palámque fit pastóribus
Pastor, creátor ómnium.

Iesu, tibi sit glória,
qui natus es de Vírgine,
cum Patre et almo Spíritu,
in sempitérna sæcula.
Amen.

THE ANNOUNCEMENT
TO THE SHEPHERDS

*Helpless he lay in a manger; glorious he shone
in the heavens. Humbled, he lived among men; eternal he dwelt
with the Father.*

The Gospel begins with two annunciations, the first to Mary, most blessed among women, and the second, nine months later, to the shepherds keeping watch at night over the flocks near Bethlehem. These two annunciations start with the same counsel: *"Do not be afraid!"* (Lk 1:30; 2:10) For, indeed, this is not a God threatening to man that manifests himself, but the God of Love. In both cases, the angel of the Lord announces very good news, indeed, the best news that could ever be announced to the world. The first announcement was reserved for the Immaculate Heart of Mary. But on Christmas night, the announcement of great joy is for all people: *"Today in the town of David a savior has been born to you; he is Christ the Lord"* (Lk 2:11).

If God sends us a Savior, it is because we are in need of saving. That is the very foundation of Christianity. Saved from what? Saved from sin, which is the cause of all our ills. Saved from sin, which makes the human condition a tragic one. Because of sin, evil, suffering, pain, anguish, fears, aging, physical and mental decline, and, ultimately, death, are the worldly lot of humanity; and, unspeakably worse, the condemnation and damnation it risks as eternal retribution. So, yes, in the words of a traditional French carol: "O come, divine Messiah, give us hope and save us!"

But this much hoped-for Messiah, how are we to find and recognize him? *"Here is a sign for you: you will find a baby wrapped in swaddling clothes and lying in a manger"* (Lk 2:12). And so we run to this Savior who has just been born, and what do we find? A human being, insignificant in all his weakness. What a disappointment! Oh, what a fine figure, this Savior of ours, with his human nature just as frail as ours! Perhaps if he had been born in a palace, the heir of a rich and powerful king. But no, he is born weak and poor. Our liberator, defenseless! Our physician, himself infirm! Our Savior appears to us completely incapable of saving even himself! And yet, the angel of the Lord cannot be mistaken: the sign that is given us affirms without a shadow of a doubt that Jesus is our Savior. The Son of God could have raised up the human nature from its fall without becoming man. But should he not first take on our fallen human nature himself in order to raise it up, in himself, to the right hand of the Father?

TIBI, CHRISTE

Thee, O Christ, the Father's splendor,
　　life and virtue of the heart,
in the presence of the angels
sing we now with tuneful art,
meetly in alternate chorus,
bearing our responsive part.

Thus we praise with veneration
all the armies of the sky;
chiefly him, the warrior primate,
o celestial chivalry,
Michael, who in princely virtue
cast Abaddon from on high.

By whose watchful care repelling—
King of everlasting grace—
every ghostly adversary,
all things evil, all things base,
grant us of thine only goodness,
in thy paradise a place.

Laud and honor to the Father,
laud and honor to the Son,
laud and honor to the Spirit,
ever Three, and ever One,
consubstantial, coeternal,
while unending ages run. Amen.

Tibi, Christe, splendor Patris,
　　vita, virtus córdium,
in conspéctu angelórum votis,
voce psállimus; alternántes
concrepándo melos damus
vócibus.

Collaudámus venerántes
ínclitos archángelos,
sed præcípue primátem
cæléstis exércitus,
Michaélem in virtúte
conteréntem Sátanam.

Quo custóde procul pelle,
rex Christe piíssime,
omne nefas inimíci;
mundos corde et córpore
paradíso redde tuo
nos sola cleméntia.

Glóriam Patri melódis
personémus vócibus,
Glóriam Christo canámus,
Glóriam Paráclito,
Qui Deus trinus et unus
Exstat ante sæcula. Amen.

THE CHOIR OF ANGELS

At the Lord's birth the choir of angels sang: Blessed be our God enthroned as King and blessed be the Lamb.

The choir of angels sings: The glory of God in the highest heaven is the peace on earth for those he loves. And not just any peace, but that peace which the Prince of Peace comes to make known and spread. What, in truth, is this peace? The peace of Christ is the peace of man with God through the remission of sins, the peace between men through the commandment of love, and the peace of man with himself with the participation of all his yearnings to desire the good that God wants. And what God wants is the happiness of all men, whom he holds dear. God wants his beloved to be blessed. And when this benevolent design is realized, God is glorified!

At Christmas, the heavenly angels sing to the glory of God not only because the Prince of Peace was made man and came to live on earth, but also because his triumph is inevitable. And yet, in a few days, the forces of evil will make war on the Prince of Peace, massacring the most innocent of innocents! And yet, for thirty-three years, the forces of evil will never cease waging war on him, and will believe they have definitively won the war. At the end of a wondrous life, in which both the weakness of his human condition and the might of his divinity were fully manifest, at the end of a life punctuated by a thousand victories over evil and death, the Prince of Peace was to be condemned and put to death on a cross. In this sense, the swaddling clothes of Jesus are the prefigurement of his shroud. True man, the Son of God did not spare his spirit any of the sorrow nor the anxiety, the wearisomeness nor the most cruel apprehensions. He rejected none of the constraints of human nature: neither hunger, thirst, fatique, suffering, nor, ultimately, death. Like one of us, Jesus was born to die; but, like God, he dies to rise again. True man, he submits to death; but, true God, death cannot hold him. This is why, at Christmas, the angels sing that henceforth God is glorified by what has happened on earth! The joy of Christmas flows from the same source as that of the *Exsultet* on Easter night. In the highest heavens, the angels know that in Jesus Christ, Savior of the world, the life and death of God on earth will mark the definitive victory of humanity over the forces of evil.

Benozzo Gozzoli (c. 1420–1497), *Angels in Adoration* (1459–1461), north wall of the cycle "Journey of the Magi," fresco, Chapel of the Magi, Medici Riccardi Palace, Florence

A student of Fra Angelico, Gozzoli was the author of several fresco cycles, including this splendid decor for the chapel of the Magi in Florence's Medici Palace.

Creatures of a spiritual essence, the angels form the link between God and man, between heaven and earth, between the visible and the invisible. Messengers of God, they also ensure perpetual adoration around the throne of God, surrounding him with their praises. It is that song of praise that is sung here by the celestial host. Borrowing a technique from his master, the painter has inscribed the haloes of the figures in the foreground with the canticle from Luke the Evangelist's account of the Nativity: *Gloria in excelsis deo…* as well as the words we sing in the liturgical hymn it inspired: *Adoramus te, glorificamus te…*.

The individualized expressions of each face, the varied poses, and the vivid colors of their clothing add remarkable depth to the composition. Our gaze, deliciously lost in the details of this charming landscape, then rises to the delicately-winged cherubim and seraphim swirling over this luxuriant countryside, enhanced by perfectly masterful perspective. There angels frolic as they gather rosebuds to weave elegant garlands. *Let us go then*, they tell us, like the shepherds *to Bethlehem and see this thing that has happened which the Lord has made known to us* (Lk 2:15).

VOX CLARA
ECCE INTONAT

hark! a herald voice is calling:
"Christ is nigh," it seems to say;
"cast away the dreams of darkness,
o ye children of the day!"

Startled at the solemn warning,
let the earth-bound soul arise;
Christ, her Sun, all sloth dispelling,
shines upon the morning skies.

Lo! the Lamb, so long expected,
comes with pardon down from heaven;
let us haste, with tears of sorrow,
one and all to be forgiven;

So when next he comes with glory,
wrapping all the earth in fear,
may he then as our defender
of the clouds of heaven appear.

Honor, glory, virtue, merit,
to the Father and the Son,
with the coeternal Spirit,
while unending ages run. Amen.

Vox clara ecce íntonat
obscura quæque increpat:
procul fugéntur sómnia;
ab æthere Christus prómicat.

Mens iam resúrgat tórpida,
quæ sorde exstat sáucia;
sidus refúlget iam novum,
ut tollat omne nóxium.

E sursum Agnus míttitur
laxáre gratis débitum;
omnes pro indulgéntia
vocem demus cum lácrimis.

Secúndo ut cum fúlserit,
mundúmque horror cínxerit,
non pro reátu púniat,
sed nos pius tunc prótegat.

Summo Parénti glória
Natóque sit victória,
et Flámini laus débita
per sæculórum sæcula. Amen.

THE ADORATION
OF THE SHEPHERDS

*The shepherds said to one another: Let us make our way
to Bethlehem and see for ourselves this thing
which the Lord has revealed to us.*

The shepherds found the newborn Jesus according to the sign the angel gave them. They recognized him immediately as one of their own, a member of the noble brotherhood of the poor, the meek and humble of heart. It is no surprise to them that the Anointed One of God should be the fruit of love and humility. For their simple lives had taught them that it is from this source alone that that which is good, that which is perfect, flows. Let us not desire particularly to be rich and famous, for therein we risk losing, along with faith in the triumph of humility, the image of divine wisdom we bear within us. And, having spent our life amassing dignity upon dignity and possession upon possession, we will then necessarily have to detach ourselves from them and be ready to lose them if we wish to be able to have the honor of calling ourselves Christians. So, what is the point, if not for the sole purpose of being of service to others? For a Christian, if destitution is a scandal crying out to the Father, poverty is an eminent dignity and the most enviable of estates.

Having adored the Child Jesus, the shepherds returned home singing to the glory of God with the hymn the angels taught them, communicating their joy to all those whom they encountered. These were thus the first apostles of Christ. And yet, *the child's father and mother stood there wondering at the things that were being said about him*" (Lk 2:33). How can we express what Mary and Joseph must have lived over the course of these events? Perhaps we would do best to imitate the silence of their contemplation. At the sight of the wonders God works for us men and for our salvation, human words fail. And so, contemplation, which turns the soul to its innermost depths wherein God dwells, gains our access to a knowledge beyond all expression. Let us read the Gospel story again, and, in the silence of our hearts, adore the mystery of the Nativity.

Fray Juan Bautista Maíno (1581–1649), *The Adoration of the Shepherds* (1612–1614), oil on canvas, 123.7 x 66.6 in.

One could almost receive this work as an invitation to a dance, a dance that leads these figures—and the viewer—to adoration. For indeed, this canvas, commissioned for the main altarpiece of the Church of San Pedro Mártir in Toledo, follows the principles of Baroque art. The credibility in the rendering of the characters and the decor, and the spontaneity and diversity of the poses, allow us to enter, naturally and with delight, into this scene wonderfully set in everyday life. The elongated format of the canvas as well as the elevated vanishing point help to assure a sense of real space within the fictional confines of the painting. This three-dimensional aspect accents the figures of the shepherds and the animals in the foreground.

The wealth of poses and facial types is admirable, as well as the naturalism of the clothing, expressions, and appearances—such as the dirty feet of the flute-player and the surprised or loving looks of the angels—all worthy of works by Caravaggio or Gentileschi, whom the artist met during his stay in Italy. Who could resist the tender gesture of Joseph kissing the chubby hand of the divine Child? Not to mention the elements of the decor and the animals, some of which, like the donkey and the ox, are absorbed in contemplation of the scene. Others play a symbolic role inherited from the early days of the Church: the lamb, recalling at one and the same time the redeeming act of Jesus, his sacrifice, and the famous words of John the Baptist: *Look, there is the lamb of God* (Jn 1:29); and the basket of eggs, the symbols of life and death.

Through light-hearted models drawn from everyday life, the interpretation by a talented colorist, and elements of still life that go well beyond the simply decorative, we seem to hear the tidings announced to the shepherds: *Do not be afraid. Listen, I bring you news of great joy, a joy to be shared by the whole people. Today in the town of David a savior has been born to you; he is Christ the Lord* (Lk 2:10-11).

QUICUMQUE CHRISTUM QUÆRITIS

All you who seek the gentle Christ,
to heaven lift your eyes and see
the sign of glory without end,
revealing his descent to earth.

this gleaming star outshines by far
the brightness of the sun's full glow,
for it declares that God made Man
has come to bless and save us all.

Behold, three sages from the East,
the lands of sunrise and of hope,
perceive the standard of the King,
and its good tidings read aright.

All glory, Jesus, be to you
revealed to all the nations now,
to God the Father glory be
and to the Spirit endlessly. Amen.

Quicúmque Christum
quæritis, óculos in altum
tóllite: illic licébit visere signum
perénnis glóriæ.

Hæc stella, quæ solis rotam
vincit decóre ac lúmine,
venísse terris núntiat cum
carne terréstri Deum.

En Pérsici ex orbis sinu,
sol unde sumit iánuam,
cernunt períti intérpretes
regále vexíllum magi.

Iesu, tibi sit glória, qui te
revélas géntibus, cum Patre
et almo Spíritu, in sempitérna
sæcula. Amen.

THE PILGRIMAGE
OF THE MAGI

*Seeing the star, the wise men said: This must signify the birth
of some great king. Let us search for him and lay our treasures
at his feet: gold, frankincense and myrrh.*

Abraham Cresques, *The Three Kings of the Orient Leave Tarsus on Horseback to Follow the Star of Bethlehem* (1375), from a Catalan world atlas, parchment, 12.6 x 59 in.

This illustration forms part of a collection of six folios attributed to Majorcan mapmaker Abraham Cresques. An exceptional document, it was one of the jewels of the royal library founded at the Louvre by Charles V in 1368. This parchment contains a description of the eastern parts of the world, with numerous allusions to religions as well as to stories of explorations known at the time, particularly Marco Polo's *Book of Wonders* and John Mandeville's *Travels*. The representation is midway between the medieval *mappae mundi* and navigational charts known as *portolans*. From the province of Colombo to the Empire of Sarra, the map mentions episodes from the Bible: the tower of Babel, Noah's ark, Nineveh, the queen of Sheba. In the center, the three Magi head west, leaving behind vast and opulent empires. They are easily recognizable, perched on their mounts, each with distinctive markings. They are on their way, guided by a star pointed out by the lead rider. Their long voyage will take them across many lands. Peaks, highlands, and mountain ranges are represented by mounds of rocky blocks piled up like ears of corn, while cities are depicted by a sometimes crenellated rampart with arrow-slits and a gate, from which rises an onion-domed tower, thus indicating pagan lands. The height of exoticism, an elephant is followed by a man whipping him on. The incorrect proportion between man and beast is perhaps evidence that the artist knew of elephants only through stories that omitted any reference to its size.

Who are the Magi? No doubt great lords, wise men, and philosophers as much as learned observers of the stars. Where did they come from? We traditionally like to think that they came from lands far distant from one another, that they set off separately, and met in a caravanserai as they entered Judea. One is supposed to have come from China, the second from India, and the third from Africa. Yet, since they were searching for the king of the Jews, they must some way or other have had access to holy Scripture, a fact that would argue for more nearby countries known to have had contact with Jewish culture: Persia, Armenia, or Abyssinia, for example. One of Isaiah's prophecies refers to them as kings of Arabia, Egypt, Chaldea, and other more distant lands. In fact, there is nothing to say that there were only three Magi, apart from the suggestion of the number of their gifts. Whatever the case, the arrival of the Magi signifies that the birth of the Messiah—having been announced to Israel in the form of those most humble representatives, the shepherds—is shared with the whole world in all its diversity, symbolized by the wise kings said to be of every race and from all four corners of the world. Thus is affirmed the universal dimension of the mission of the Savior of the world.

The Gospel explains to us why these important figures decided to undertake their long journey. Having observed the appearance of a new star in the skies, a star whose trajectory was toward Jerusalem, they followed. So they knew that this star was to appear to hail the birth of the king of the Jews, perhaps through the prophecy of Balaam, a prophet among the pagans, taken up by their own traditions. Balaam had seen the Savior of the world appear like a star and foretold: *A star from Jacob takes the leadership, a scepter arises from Israel* (cf. Nm 24:17). The actions of these learned men attest that science, in its research into the truths of nature, is not opposed to faith but, on the contrary, can lead to God: truth by truth, objective knowledge leads us toward God who is the Truth of truths.

But for such wise people to decide to undertake such a pilgrimage, following a heavenly sign, it was necessary that God simultaneously raise up a star in their hearts. As much as by a visible star, the Magi were moved to the depths of their beings by an inspiration of the Holy Spirit. So it is for us: when God sends an external sign that overwhelms us, he makes our hearts burn to respond by leaving behind the routines of our existence and setting off on the road toward Jesus Christ.

Lord Frederic Leighton (1830–1896), *The Star of Bethlehem* (c. 1862), oil on canvas, 61 x 23.3 in.

From the terrace of his dwelling, he sees the rising of a star that will set him and his companions off on a journey. This is a king, as indicated by the crown he rather nonchalantly holds in his hand. In this moment, his title and function little matter. What matters is to respond to a call, to an imperious desire: to go to meet the one true King of the universe. *"Where is the infant king of the Jews?"* he will ask upon arrival in Jerusalem at the end of a long voyage. *"We saw his star as it rose and have come to do him homage"* (Mt 2:2). But let's not get ahead of ourselves…. For the moment, he stares at this star, as dazzling as the sun. A spark of its light glints in his eye. Its brightness seems to excite in him the firm resolution to depart. For in spirit he has already set off, has already plunged into the incredible odyssey that will lead him to bow down before the one true God. The striking low-angle view gives us the impression of intruding upon the private reveries of this massive and majestic sculptural figure. Enveloped in traditional oriental garb, this full-bearded king is commanding. And yet he exudes a profound sensitivity. Don't make a sound; let's not disturb his meditation, but rather join in his goal. For into each one of our lives a providential star is rising, the sign of the epiphany of Jesus the Savior.

For the commentary on the fresco below, *The Star of Balaam*, see page 122.

HOSTIS HERODES IMPIE

Why should the wicked Herod fear the coming of the Savior, Christ? He will not plunder earthly realms, who gives a Kingdom from above.

The Eastern sages followed on as shining Star preceded them. By means of light, true Light they sought, and off'ring gifts, their God adored.

The spotless Lamb from God's high throne required of John to baptize him: in Jordan's waters cleansing thus his people's sin, though sinless he.

All praise and glory, Lord, be yours, who showed yourself to men this day: all honor to the Father, too, and Holy Spirit, Three in One. Amen.

hostis Heródes ímpie, Christum veníre quid times? Non éripit mortália qui regna dat cæléstia.

Ibant Magi, qua vénerant stellam sequéntes præviam, lumen requírunt lúmine, Deum faténtur múnere.

Lavácra puri gúrgitis cæléstis Agnus attigit; peccáta quæ non détulit nos abluéndo sústulit.

Iesu, tibi sit glória, qui te relévas géntibus, cum Patre et almo Spíritu, in sempitérna sæcula. Amen.

THE MAGI VISIT
HEROD

*Herod questioned the Magi: What is this sign of which you
speak, this sign of a newborn king? We saw a brilliant
star in the heavens; its splendor filled the world.*

Toward the end of a brilliant reign begun a good three decades earlier in 37 BC, the king of the Jews, Herod I, called "the Great," was suffering from an incurable illness, which was soon to carry him off. Obsessed by the question of his succession, he was endlessly occupied in thwarting the intrigues and plots, real and imagined, fomented by his entourage.

Herod's reign had made its mark on the times well beyond the land of the Jews. Had he not even restored the Olympic Games, fallen into neglect, and been named its President for life? A monarch as hard as he was clever, at the price of the bloody sacrifice of the subjects of his realm, he had entered the homeland of the Jews into the modern Greco-Roman world. The language of its administration became Greek, and a number of towns, rebuilt or newly established, rivalled Hellenistic cities in splendor: paved thoroughfares, porticos and aquaducts, theaters and palaces, hippodromes, circuses, even amphitheaters witnessed to a fast-paced shift to the way of life of pagan civilization.

To the great scandal of Jews faithful to the religion of their fathers, these new urban centers even welcomed Dionysian guilds and troops of gladiators. The Roman Empire, of which Augustus was then the absolute master, appreciated the collaboration and unfaltering "friendship" of this vassal king. But Herod also knew how to placate the pious nationalist Jews, notably by reconstructing a grandiose temple in Jerusalem that would be counted among the wonders of the ancient world, and by reestablishing the ancestral cult of the royal sanctuary founded by David and carried out by Solomon.

And so it was to this powerful and morbidly jealous king that the Magi traveled from the Orient, to consult and discover where the King of the Jews was to be born—for the star that had guided them was hidden somewhere in the skies above Jerusalem. The Scriptures were a sufficient light to illuminate the Jews, and directed them with confidence to the Messiah who was to be born among them. With no hesitation, the chief priests and doctors of the Law shone this light of prophetic truth: the new David was to be born in Bethlehem of Judea, according to the words of the prophet Micah (cf. Mi 5:1).

Against all expectation, Herod was no more furious with the Magi than with the sages of Israel. Touched to the quick, as an astute strategist, he decided to pardon these prophets of doom, the better to target the real object of his irascible jealousy. *"Go and find out all about the child,* he told the Magi, *and when you have found him, let me know, so that that I too may go and do him homage"* (Mt 2:8). This cruel man's sole concern was to find this mysterious rival come to threaten his glorious career—only in order to do away with him. How pointless all his dissimulated terrors! For Herod had nothing to fear from this new King, this Prince of peace whose kingdom is not of this world. Thus is ambition itself ever the scourge of the ambitious.

The Magi before Herod (1230–1240), detail of the stained-glass window of the Life of the Virgin, Cathedral of Saint-Étienne, Sens, France

We are present at a summit meeting between four kings. At the moment we happen upon this conversation, discussions are well underway between the standing Caspar, Melchior, Balthazar, and the enthroned Herod. An ancient tradition associated the three Magi with the three parts of the then-known world (Asia, Africa, and Europe), but also—as here—with the three ages of man. They bear royal attributes (crowns and mantles), and hold their gifts in containers of precious metals. The youngest of the three foreigners points to the sky with his right hand, indicating the star that has led them all the way to Palestine. *"'Where is the infant king of the Jews?' they asked. 'We saw his star as it rose and have come to do him homage.'"* (Mt 2:2). The Evangelist records that Herod was greatly troubled upon hearing this, and we can read a hint of worry on his face. He echoes the gesture of the young man, pointing in the same direction to underscore the import of his reply: *"'Go and find out all about the child,' he said, 'and when you have found him, let me know, so that I too may go out and do him homage.'"* (Mt 2:8).

But his words are no more than a ruse. The sword in his hand, like a menacing slash in the center of the composition, already forbodes ignoble intentions.

As with so many of these thirteenth-century creations, we marvel at the quality of the colors (especially the variations of blue and the gradation of the tones of the costumes) and are charmed by the talent of these master glassmakers, experts in the art of the harmonious arrangement of figures, all within the circular space of a medallion.

QUIS ISTE TANTUS

"What is this marvelous thing,"
    they say,
"A king who thus commands the stars,
Whom pow'rs above adore in fear,
Whom light and heaven's realm obey?

For we perceive a glory new,
Transcendent, endless and sublime,
Far older than the skies above,
Unfathomed by the dark abyss.

He is the King of nations all,
Expected by the Jews of old,
The promised seed of Abraham,
Born of his race in course of time."

Quis iste tantus,
    ínquiunt,
regnátor astris ímperans,
Quem sic tremunt cæléstia,
cui lux et æthra insérviunt ?

Illústre quiddam cérnimus,
quod nésciat finem pati,
sublíme, celsum, intérminum,
antíquius cælo et chao.

Hic ille rex est géntium
populíque rex Iudáici,
promíssus Abrahæ patri
eiúsque in ævum sémini.

THE ADORATION
OF THE MAGI

*The wise men came from the East to adore the Lord
in Bethlehem. Opening their treasures, they offered him three
precious gifts: gold for the great King, frankincense
for the true God, and myrrh for his burial, alleluia.*

After the Magi had submitted to the light of Scripture by setting off on the road to Bethlehem, the star reappeared and came to a halt over a shelter in which the Child lay. There they prostrated themselves in adoration and offered him gold, frankincense, and myrrh: gold, the tribute in honor of the royalty of the Anointed One of God; incense, to glorify the divinity of the Only Begotten Son; myrrh, a perfume used to embalm the dead, in veneration of the humanity of our mortal brother.

And as for us, what do we offer Jesus? What is the gold that the Christian lays before the child Jesus? The Christian's gold, gold refined by fire, as Revelation tells us (cf. Rv 3:18), is love. But how can we procure this love? Love is purchased through love itself: by loving we amass love! Because it is God who first loved us, it is only at the price of the love of others that we may purchase the love of God (cf. 1 Jn). Only when we are able to offer this gold of love may we add the incense: a life of prayer that rises to God like a fragrant aroma, because it is unalloyed by hypocrisy. But the incense of our prayers is nothing without the myrrh, that is, without participation in the Passion and Death of Christ. The myrrh in our lives is our sufferings, our sacrifices, and our death, offered in communion with the Eucharist of the Lord. In this sense, when we love as Jesus Christ loved us, when we give the greatest proof of love, our life offered for those we love, through a divine alchemy the myrrh transmutes us into gold refined by fire, making of our lives an incense pleasing to God.

Thus did David pray, *"In these rich offerings, Lord, we offer you nothing more than what we have received from your hands"* (cf. Chr 29:14). In truth, the only gifts that we can offer that are at the same time worthy of us and worthy of God are those with which the Child Jesus came to shower us. In measure beyond measure, he came to share with us the gold of his love for his own who are in the world. In measure beyond measure, he came to give us the Holy Spirit, who enters into our hearts to cry out, *Abba*, Father, in ineffable prayers. In measure beyond measure, he came to hand over his body for us and to spill his blood for us in order to grant us communion in his Death and Resurrection.

Giambattista Tiepolo (1696–1770), *The Adoration of the Magi* (1753), oil on canvas, 160 x 82.7 in.

"Going into the house they saw the child with his mother Mary, and falling to their knees they did him homage. Then, opening their treasures, they offered him gifts of gold and frankincense and myrrh" (Mt 2:11). The Evangelist does not specify the number of Magi, nor their names. Their number has generally been fixed at three since Origen (185–224), and it seems to have been Tertullian (c. 160–230) who first identified the Magi as kings, in reference to the Psalms (68:30; 72:10). Mary is seated in front of Joseph, slightly to the left of a tightly packed arrangement of the figures' heads. On her lap sits the child, turning his eyes to the face of the elderly king, who bows in veneration, his hands joined. A tête-à-tête interplay of intense gazes is established.

In this composition, Tiepolo's great originality lies in the presentation of the other kings in the background, crowded behind their companion. With their backs to us and framing the scene, a servant, his right elbow jutting out to accentuate depth, and a page of the royal retinue, increase the scale of the figures, heightening the viewer's impression of proximity to the scene.

For once, the gifts take second stage, for the hands bearing the precious vase are anonymous, and the presence of the ox is suggested by just one of its horns. The main figures are highlighted through a staging far removed from simple narrative. The stone wall serves as a loggia, marking the separation between what remains of the family's privacy and the group of onlookers. Applied in large patches, the colors have a crispness that accentuates the light typical of the Venetian style, of which Tiepolo was the greatest eighteenth-century proponent.

AUDIT TYRANNUS
ANXIUS

The anxious tyrant's troubled ears
  Have heard that there is born
the King,
Appointed to fill David's place
and rule the land of Israel.

In guilty madness he exclaims:
"We must protect our threatened throne!
Go, servant, draw a ruthless sword,
And stain the cradles red with blood."

What profit brings this craven deed?
Where, cruel Herod, is your gain?
In safety from your evil schemes
The Infant Christ is borne away.

Audit tyránnus ánxius
  adésse regum
príncipem,
qui nomen Israel regat
teneátque David régiam.

Exclámat amens núntio:
"Succéssor instat, péllimur;
satélles, i, ferrum rape,
perfúnde cunas sánguine!"

Quo próficit tantum nefas?
Quid crimen Heródem iuvat?
Unus tot inter fúnera
impúne Christus tóllitur.

THE FLIGHT INTO EGYPT

Joseph rose in the night and took the child and his mother into
Egypt. There they stayed until the death of Herod,
alleluia.

After worshiping the Child, the Magi, warned in a dream not to return to Herod, left for their countries, bypassing Jerusalem. Joseph, also warned of the deadly designs of the great king, took the mother and Child and, secretly, all three fled to Egypt.

From infancy, the Son of God found himself caught up in the unfolding drama that is all human existence. But Jesus' parents had already discovered that, for their Child, life would be a daily fight to ward off the fatal outcome. True man, in receiving life, Jesus also received the heritage of death. This death threat, beginning with Herod's, would remain a constant throughout his earthly existence; tragedy would run though his life as though in enflamed battle between good and evil.

Suffering and death were therefore for Jesus a never-ending prospect, beginning with the massacre of the children in Bethlehem and confirmed by the execution of John, his precursor even in death. And yet, in the life of Jesus, a fatal ending never appeared as a road with no way out. Already in the flight into Egypt, Jesus escaped the homicidal madness of the tyrant; already the light refused to be extinguished by the darkness; already life was victorious over death.

Soon the words and deeds of Jesus would reclaim the drama of life, not as an occasion for a call to stoicism or heroism, still less to relativism or to diversions, but as the first tragic act in a story that ends well—a happy ending promised not to Jesus alone, but promised to all, as a personal possession, a grace, conferred through him on the entire human condition. Thus, in the same way that Jesus, following the patriarchs Abraham and Joseph, found salvation in Egypt, so too does human existence find its salvation—not in miraculously rediscovering a state of perfection before death, nor by escaping death, but by passing, through the baptism of death, from the kingdom of the Prince of this world into the Kingdom of God.

Henry Ossawa Tanner (1859–1937), *The Flight into Egypt* (1923), oil on canvas, 29 x 26 in.

Danger is afoot. With the warning ringing in Joseph's ears, they must depart without delay. In the depths of the night in this sleeping town, it is not an angel who helps the Holy Family to flee, but an anonymous man, highlighting the importance of mutual aid and brotherhood. All must take place with the greatest discretion; we might rightly infer that they are furtively skirting the walls. In the heart of what we recognize as the street of a medina, we contemplate this young mother clasping her slumbering newborn in her arms, prey to a wholly justified fear.

The guide's lantern, the sole source of light, intensifies the relief of the large doorway, which will remain closed once they have gone, and projects Mary's shadow onto the wall. The great archway opening onto the night sky heralds a departure into the unknown.

This African-American artist, who joined the American Art Students Club in Paris, makes use of the sparse fifth-century style of iconography, before the medium began to achieve greater complexity by the addition of new characters. We feel here to what extent, since the day of his birth, *the Son of Man has nowhere to lay his head* (Mt 8:20). But, since they are moving toward us, this is also an invitation to welcome the Savior, not in the faraway land of Egypt, but in our hearts and in the very core of our lives.

SALVETE FLORES
MARTYRUM

ᚼail, fairest flow'rs of martyrdom,
    sweet roses in their earthly bud,
but plucked by enemy of Christ,
when on the threshold of your life.

A little flock of tender lambs,
you were the first oblations pure;
beneath the altar-throne of Christ
you gaily play with palms and crowns.

All glory, Jesus, be to you
born of a Virgin undefiled,
who with the Spirit of your Love
and God the Father, ever reign. Amen.

Ꙃalvéte, flores mártyrum,
    quos lucis ipso in límine
Christi insecútor sústulit
ceu turbo nascéntes rosas.

Vos prima Christi víctima,
grex immolatórum tener,
aram sub ipsam símplices
palma et corónis lúditis.

Iesu, tibi sit glória, qui natus
es de Vírgine, cum Patre et
almo Spíritu, in sempitérna
sæcula. Amen.

THE MASSACRE
OF THE HOLY INNOCENTS

*At the king's command these innocent babies and little children
were put to death; they died for Christ, and now in the glory
of heaven as they follow him, the sinless Lamb, they sing for ever:
Glory to you, O Lord.*

In this world, we are in a bit of the same situation as the Magi and Herod. They were all seeking the baby Jesus: the former to adore him, the latter to kill him. But none of them seemed to have the slightest chance of finding him. To go find a little child born in the hay, when you are looking for a king—and the King of kings at that! Fortunately for the Magi, they were guided by a star that came to rest over the place where the Infant lay. As for Herod, unwilling to let himself be guided toward Jesus, much less to find and recognize him, there was no other way of being sure he had done away with him than to have all the newborns in the district of Bethlehem killed.

So today, we find ourselves in a similar situation to theirs: we seek Jesus to worship before him like the Magi—not, of course, to kill him like Herod, but rather to love him. We do not have much trouble in finding him in order to worship him, for the Church lights a little red star for us above the place where Jesus lies, really and truly present in the form of the sacred Host. But in order to love him? We can only truly love—not in word or speech, but in deed and truth (cf. 1 Jn 3:18)—a real person whom we actually meet and with whom we form a true and unique personal relationship in real life. If not, we risk loving only a dream, a mental construct of our own making, which does not correspond to any real living person. So how can we be certain to have found the living person of Jesus in our lives, in order to love him? Well, to find Jesus and love him, really and truly, I dare say we must make ourselves Herods of love. Just as Herod was obliged to kill all the newborns in order to kill Jesus, in the same way, in order to be sure of loving Jesus, we must love all those that God places in our path through life. For no other criterion has been given us to recognize his presence in our lives than this: he became one among us. This is the historic fact that we celebrate at Christmas: in his manifestation to the world, God did not want us to find, recognize, and love him through the expression of his divinity. And thus it was an infinite grace he bestowed upon us. To his Jewish contemporaries, this was the sign of the accomplishment of the Law in its fullness. For us Christians, it was the condition for the gift of the Eucharist and the new commandment.

Guido Reni (1575–1642), *The Massacre of the Innocents* (1611), oil on canvas, 105.5 x 67 in.

Matthew is the only Evangelist to mention this bloody episode, which follows directly after the flight into Egypt: *"Herod was furious when he realized that he had been outwitted by the wise men, and in Bethlehem and its surrounding district he had all the male children killed who were two years old or under, reckoning by the date he had been careful to ask the wise men"* (Mt 2:16).

While in medieval depictions Herod presides over the massacre, here the painter opts to concentrate on the tragedy, focusing on a storm of violence and terror. The two large lateral figures take to flight in a vain attempt to save themselves. Just as vain are the supplications of the kneeling woman in the center background, and the evasive movement of the woman on her knees at the feet of an executioner set upon stabbing the sharp blade of his dagger in the hearts of these little innocents. Through this abundance of figures, the disparity of poses, and the variety of expressions, cries seem to reach our ears as the soldiers thrust out their powerful arms like lightning.

The theatricality typical of the Baroque movement, of which Reni was one of the worthiest representatives, does not hamper the reading of this work. Thanks to a rigorous composition that avoids clutter or confusion, we are able to appreciate each detail well beyond our status as simple spectators. We are plunged into the heart of the drama; we share in the grief of this distraught mother in the foreground, on her knees, broken but dignified, her eyes raised to the heavens with hands joined before her child's corpse—a veritable *pietà*. In the depths of her sorrow, she is henceforth alone amid the tumult and the crowd.

O LUX BEATA CÆLITUM

O Jesus, light of heaven's joy,
and highest hope of mortal man,
the purest love that home can know
surrounded your frail infancy.

O Mary, rich in every grace,
your privilege was quite unique,
to feed your Son and Infant God,
and softly kiss his tiny cheek.

Most honored patriarch of all,
the Virgin Mother's strength and stay,
the chosen guardian of your Lord,
who called you Father day by day.

All three from Jesse's noble stem,
and born to do salvation's work,
pay heed to all the earnest prayers
we trustfully pour out to you.

As your home flourished with the grace
of every virtue's fairest flow'r,
in love and peace may all our homes
reflect a little of your own.

O Jesus, most obedient
to those who held true parents' place,
all praise to you who reign on high
in Godhead's perfect Trinity. Amen.

O lux beáta cælitum
et summa spes
mortálium, Iesu, o cui
doméstica arrísit orto cáritas;

María, dives grátia,
o sola quæ casto potes
fovére Iesum péctore,
cum lacte donans óscula;

Tuque ex vetústis pátribus
delécte custos Vírginis,
dulci patris quem nómine
divína Proles ínvocat:

De stirpe Iesse nóbili
nati in salútem géntium,
audíte nos, qui súpplices
ex corde vota fúndimus.

Qua vestra sedes flóruit
virtútis omnis grátia,
hanc detur in domésticis
reférre posse móribus.

Iesu, tuis obœdiens
qui factus es paréntibus,
cum Patre summo ac Spíritu
semper tibi sit glória. Amen.

THE HOLY FAMILY
IN NAZARETH

Lord, give us light through the example of your family and guide
our feet into the way of peace.

After their short exile in Egypt, immediately upon the death of Herod in the year 4 BC, the Holy Family returned to live in the heart of Galilee, the crossroads of nations, in Nazareth, the town they came from. Jesus grew up there, learning the carpenter's trade at his father Joseph's side. The family business would undoubtedly have been enjoying flourishing trade at the time, participating in the development of the powerful and sumptuous city of Sephoris, the largely new town that Herod Antipas, upon succeeding his father, had decided to build as his capital. This city where, according to tradition, Joachim and Anne, the parents of Mary, lived, was located some three miles from Nazareth. Jesus was therefore a priviliged eyewitness to the way this second-generation Herod continued his father's pagan-friendly policy. His youth was steeped in a Western Greco-Roman culture enhanced by unprecedented economic development. But the circle of his extended family would also have jealously guarded the young Jesus within the confines of the Jewish community that nurtured him with the ancestral life-blood.

Thus, in Nazareth, the Son of Man spent thirty years of his earthly life living hidden among his family. Little is known of this period of his life beyond the fact that he lived humbly, in submission to his parents' ordinary vocation of marriage. And yet, if there is nothing remarkable in that, it can never be

The Childhood of Jesus (17th c.), engraving.

This engraving calls to mind the lovely stories our parents and grandparents told us. Many readers who are or who have been happy parents will delight to find here these scenes of family life and of the development of the little Child from the cradle to his first steps.

The juxtaposition of episodes begins in the upper left with a small group of angel musicians lulling the Newborn to sleep with their song and their music. Not just anyone enjoys such company: Jesus is the Son of God! Time passes. In the lower left, Mary encourages her Son to take his first steps. He has nothing to fear; he can go ahead, for Joseph is waiting for him, leaning toward him with outstretched arms. Looking up again to the right, we find a domestic scene with Mary, Joseph, and the Child gathered under an arbor around the family table. Before the meal, they fold their hands and give thanks to God in a touching "grace." Finally, below, Jesus good-naturedly helps his adoptive father with his carpentry work, carrying him planks of wood, while the Virgin concentrates on her needlework.

Nothing is known of the daily life of the Holy Family, but the charming anachronisms found in this illustration, which return to certain iconographic themes inherited from former ages, bring home to us all the profound humanity and closeness of the Savior.

emphasized enough that these thirty years in Nazareth were fully part of the salvific activity of Christ. Here is the paradox of the triumph of humility: the world has been saved by the hidden as well as the public life of Jesus. It was his entire life, from Mary's womb all the way to the cross, that the Son offered to his Father "for us men and for our salvation." What a prospect for all those who humbly lead their Christian lives "hidden" in the heart of their conjugal and familial vocations! As Saint Clement of Alexandria reminded married people: "Do not doubt for a moment that, like the house of the Holy Family in Nazareth, your family home, too, is a house of God."

Pietro Annigoni (1910–1988), *Saint Joseph the Worker* (1963), oil on canvas, Basilica of San Lorenzo, Florence

The skill of the artist, bolstered by his genius, combines expressivity and matter to foster a dialogue between viewer and canvas.

In this space bathed in a velvety, supernatural light, the young Jesus, with his very Westernized crop of golden hair, has joined his father in his carpentry shop. Bent over the workbench, his right hand rests on two planks of wood while he carefully examines, as though fascinated, the nails held in his left hand. With similar concentration, Joseph's chiseled face expresses both deep tenderness and profound melancholy. He is about to place his hand on the Child's head in a gesture of blessing, but also of love and comfort. He has a presentiment of the far more abominable use to be made of this wood that will form the cross and these nails that will pierce the body of his Child, the Christ, true God and true man. The rendering of the objects and tools; the depth suggested by the wooden awning; the treatment of the landscape, oscillating between the abstract gold background and figurative elements of vivid or soft colors: all enhance these two figures, lending them a noble relief and a magisterial presence. This Italian artist enables us to experience a real relationship: it is our gaze that joins with the carpenter's hand in a caress that unreservedly enters us into this poignant moment of intimacy.

For the commentary on the medallion below, *Jesus Christ and Saint John the Baptist as Children*, see page 123.

CHRISTE,
SPLENDOR PATRIS

Splendor of the Father,
Jesus Christ our Savior,
Mary Virgin Mother,
Joseph, their protector,

Family most holy,
pattern of all virtues,
shed those graces on us
which adorned your homestead.

Humble leader Joseph,
held a father's office,
teacher of the Christ Child,
serving him and Mary.

Jesus, Mary, Joseph,
grant to us the virtues
which make homelife happy,
following your model.

Christe, splendor Patris,
Dei mater Virgo,
Ioseph, tam sacrórum
pígnorum servátor,

Nitet vestra domus
flóribus virtútum,
unde gratiárum
fons prománat ipse.

Imus præes, Ioseph,
humilísque iubes;
iubes et María
et utríque servis.

Iesu, Mater, Ioseph,
mansiónis vestræ
nostras date sedes
donis frui sanctis.

JESUS IN THE TEMPLE

Your words are filled with grace,
because God has blessed you for ever.

The Gospel tells us that the Child Jesus grew in strength, wisdom, and grace, and that he was obedient to his parents (cf. Lk 2:51-52). Whether in the family or in public, at gatherings held at regular days and times, his personality was formed in the collective exercise of prayer. Jesus would chant or recite the Psalms, as his parents, immersed in the Scriptures as they were, had taught him.

To account for his future extraordinary gifts, it is supposed that he was a child prodigy, displaying a most quick-witted mind, particularly in the study of the Mosaic law, the books of the prophets, and the writings of the sages of Israel. It is also presumed that he was taught to read by the scribes and masters reputed for their subtle debate of the Law. However, the accounts of his family and neighbors seem to suggest that he pursued no particular study beyond that of the craft of carpentry: *"Where did this man get all this? What kind of wisdom has been given him?"* exclaimed childhood acquaintances (cf. Mt 13:54-56).

Jesus progressed as all other children his age and, though steeped in Greco-Roman culture—he spoke Greek as well as Aramaic—he was raised according to the traditions of the very observant Jewish middle class to which he belonged. Was he an exemplary boy in terms of human development? Of that there can be little doubt, though we cannot affirm it. But it is certain that his behavior was at times surprising, as attested by the episode when, at the age of twelve, on the return from the pilgrimage to Jerusalem, he parted company with his family.

While his parents, gripped by growing anxiety, were busy searching for him, Jesus remained in the Temple for five days to listen to the teachers of the Law—the masters of religious instruction in Israel—and ask them questions, as though compelled by an unquenchable thirst to learn of the things of God. But these luminaries of religious studies were surprised to find that it was they themselves who were enlightened. Soon the masters were listening to the student, astounded by his intelligence and his replies.

When his father and mother, having found him, reproached him for running away, they too were speechless before his answer: *"Did you not know that I must be in my Father's house?"* (Lk 2:49). Thus, of Jesus on the brink of adolescence, the only behavior and the only words known to us are the expression of the sovereign authority which would later bring others to exclaim of him: *"But who then is this man?"* (cf. Mt 8:27).

In the Prologue to the fourth Gospel, the disciple whom Jesus loved proclaims that from his conception in Mary's womb, the man Jesus was filled with a grace and truth entrusted to him by God his Father as his only Son (cf. Jn 1:14). Throughout his childhood, through the development of his physical skills and the forming of his intellectual faculties, Jesus acquired the means of expressing through his humanity this plenitude of grace and truth, in order to manifest it to the world.

Emil Nolde (1867–1956), *The Child Jesus in the Temple* (1911), from the polyptych of the *Life of Christ*, oil on canvas, 39 x 33.8 in.

The singular style of this German Expressionist painter is unsettling. His work was profoundly influenced by his discovery of the paintings of Vincent Van Gogh and Paul Gauguin, as witnessed in the broad patches of vivid color. Little matters the non-traditional representation— what counts is the very personal emotion the painter experienced before this sacred story.

The Child Jesus is engrossed in his reading of the Word of God. *"They found him in the Temple, sitting among the doctors, listening to them, and asking them questions; and all those who heard him were astounded at his intelligence and his replies"* (Lk 2:46-47). If the child astounds by his answers, if he is admired by the teachers of the law whom we see here drinking in his words, it is not because he had studiously learned the answers, but because he is in communion with his Father. He concentrates, unmindful of the reactions of these learned experts. One of them hieratically stands, while the three others form a circle of approving, admiring, and attentive faces. This work is startling and innovative. The vibrant colors draw our attention to the bodies and faces, to the energetic evocative expressions, and to the grotesque appearance of these figures. This image indeed sets the codified, tried and tested representation of this scene on its head. Nolde wished his paintings "to elevate and move, to produce within the viewer a sound full of life and humanity." And in this he succeeds, for, to say the least, he does not leave us indifferent.

O GLORIOSA DOMINA

O glorious Lady, throned in light,
  sublime above the starry height,
thine arms thy great Creator pressed,
a suckling at thy sacred breast.

Through the dear Blossom of thy womb,
thou changest hapless Eva's doom:
through thee to contrite souls is given
an opening to their home in heaven.

Thou art the great King's portal bright,
with pearls and stones of living light,
come then, ye ransomed nations, sing
the life divine 'twas hers to bring.

All glory be to thee, O Lord,
the Virgin's son, by all adored,
and equal praise forever greet,
the Father and the Paraclete. Amen.

O gloriósa Dómina,
  excélsa super sídera,
qui te creávit próvide,
lactas sacráto úbere.

Quod Eva tristis ábstulit,
tu reddis almo gérmine,
intrent ut astra flébiles,
sternis benígna sémitam.

Tu regis alti iánua
et porta lucis fúlgida;
vitam datam per Vírginem,
gentes redémptæ pláudite.

Patri sit et Paráclito
tuóque Nato glória,
qui veste te mirábili
circumdéderunt grátiæ. Amen.

THE MEDITATION
OF MARY

*We sing your praises, holy Mother of God: you gave birth
to our Savior, Jesus Christ; watch over all who honor you.*

Much more than a true story, much more than the story of truth, the story of Mary and Joseph, the story of the Holy Family, the story of God made man, is a love story. A love at first surreptitious, but which will never cease spreading its splendor in our hearts until the end of time. A love that, in the great light of day on the Last Judgment, will triumph for ever, when the love of God will be all in all.

Mary herself did not at first fully gauge the infinite importance of the "Yes!" she had spoken to Joseph, her dear sweet spouse, no more than of the *"Fiat!"* with which she replied to the announcement of the begetting of God's plan within her. The perfect model of all believers, she saw all with the eyes of faith, trusting, in everything, the Word of God. But she nevertheless could not guess what her life would be, even less what the life of her Son would be. She was no extraterrestrial robot programmed to accomplish a divine mission on earth. But neither was she a word-perfect actor playing a scene scripted in advance. Mary was a free woman—indeed, the only totally liberated woman, being untouched by sin. And she was a strong woman. Mary participated in writing a story that bears the hallmarks of her personality and of her own free will.

Mary loved. Thus, she believed all things, hoped all things, endured all things (cf. 1 Cor 13:7). But she was not adept in the science of mysteries. She who believed in the love of God for us would often ask herself, "But who, then, is my Child?" The angel Gabriel, her husband Joseph, Elizabeth her cousin, the shepherds of Bethlehem, the Magi, Herod, the aged Simeon, the prophetess Anna, her nephew John the Baptist, and many others would help her, each in their own light, to discover what concerned her Son in the Law and the Prophets. But often the Gospels affirm or suggest that Mary was amazed by what was happening, or even that she did not comprehend it.

Good mother that she was, Mary could not help but wish with all her being to protect her Child from the consequences of the most radical demands of his mission. Thus did she severely reproach him when, at the age of twelve, he withdrew to the Jerusalem Temple, and she failed to understand his explanation, clear though it was. Thus she would even take part in a family expedition traveling from Nazareth to Capernaum to try to bring the thirty-year-old Jesus back to his senses and back home (cf. Mk 3:21, 31-35).

"Who, then, is my Child?" Mary, first among all Christians and for ever the sole innate Christian, meditated on all the events in the life of Jesus in her heart. She gave thanks to God for what she did understand, adored what she did not, and never ceased repeating the *"Fiat!"* by which the Son of the Most High was begotten through her, Son of Man and firstborn of a multitude of brothers.

"Who then is my Child?" The answer would soon be told: *"Yes, God loved the world so much that he gave his only Son"* (Jn 3:16).

Page 115: **Giovanni Battista Salvi**, called **il Sassoferrato** (1609–1685), *The Virgin in Prayer* (1640–1650), oil on canvas, 28.7 x 22.7 in.

One of the painter's mature works, this is without doubt one of the most popular works in Western sacred art. Although active in the seventeenth century, Sassoferrato drew inspiration from his Renaissance predecessors Raphael and Perugino. By placing the accent on the delicately rendered fabric of the brilliant white veil and the ultramarine blue mantle, an astonishing presence seems to propel this figure out of the canvas. For the most part, her face remains in shadow, her lowered gaze a sign of intense reflection and of the profoundly moving events she has experienced. The hands joined in contemplation and prayer stand out, their gentle delicacy bathed by a beam of light descending from the top of the canvas, wich sets them in striking relief.

Despite her reserve, Mary glows. She is truly the one who *"kept all these things in her heart"* (Lk 2:51). Through his palette and the refinement of this light emerging from the darkness, Sassoferrato conveys to the viewer Mary's internal debate, a mixture of astonishment, fear, acceptance, and respect, but also of joy. The painter invites us to receive the breath of God, the better to set off in the footsteps of Christ. Through his sober, humanizing, and refined treatment, this is a major masterpiece that makes itself felt as an overwhelming presence, rich in meditative silence.

Francisco de Zurburán (1598–1664), *Christ and the Virgin in the House at Nazareth* (c. 1640), oil on canvas, 65 x 86 in.

As for so many painters, it was apocryphal texts, Jacobus de Voragine's *Golden Legend* and the *Meditations* of Pseudo-Bonaventure, that inspired this Spanish master's evocation of the childhood of Jesus. This remarkable composition of prefigurings of the Passion is set in a room of the house in Nazareth. On the left, the young boy of about twelve has just pricked his finger as he weaves a crown of thorns. He is captivated and moved by his wound. Near him sits his mother, an imposing pyramidal figure dressed in red, the color of love and martyrdom. Here, Mary is the veritable image of melancholy. Having interrupted her needlework, she regards her child, her cheek leaning on her hand, a teardrop dampening her beautiful pensive face, plunged in anxious thought. To her left, the lily symbolizes her perpetual virginity, and the carnations, the passion she will undergo as she accompanies that of her Son. Around the two protagonists, several symbols are bathed in the warm light that structures the scene. On the little table, pears symbolize the qualites of the soul of Mary: exquisiteness, sweetness, and gentleness. At the boy's feet, a terracotta bowl of pure water is an allusion to Christian baptism, whose graces will be obtained by Jesus at the cost of his baptism of death. In the lower right, the pair of turtledoves recalls the Presentation in the Temple and the tragic prophecy of the aged Simeon a few years before: *"And you yourself a sword will pierce"* (Lk 2:35). But it is salvation that will triumph over death. The large white cloth lying in Mary's lap is a shroud, the sign of the Death and Resurrection of Christ; for, through the genius of Zurbaràn, Christ tells us once again: *"And knows that, I am with you always; yes, to the end of time"* (Mt 28:20).

117

EPILOGUE

God so loved the world...

For the desert ascetics, those ancient anchorites, nuts were precious for the full meal, well protected and easy to preserve, contained within their shells. By analogy, they coined the term *Evangelium in nuce*, "the Gospel in a nutshell," to refer to the few verses from the four Gospels that they would learn by heart and upon which they would then ceaselessly meditate. Indeed, these selected verses were reputed to encapsulate within one sentence a synthesis of the entire Gospel.

Among these *Evangelii in nuce* there is one that perfectly corresponds to the splendors of Christmas, which this book invites us to contemplate: it is chapter 3, verse 16 of the fourth Gospel—words spoken by our Lord Jesus Christ himself in response to Nicodemus:
"Yes, God loved the world so much that he gave his only Son, so that everyone who believes in him may not be lost but may have eternal life."

The mystery of Christmas, the essence of the Good News of salvation, is contained within the very core of this nutshell: God is our Father and he is nothing but Love; he saves us through the Incarnation of his Son, the second Person of the Trinity, allowing us to obtain salvation through faith; escaping the horrible tragedy of condemnation ever after, we are promised to eternal happiness. All of the doctrine of the redemptive Incarnation is herein condensed. All of it? It might seem not, for one essential element is apparently missing, the new commandment. But, in reality, the commandment of Love is implicitly contained within the first phrase of this verse: *God loved the world so much* implies that we should love one another just as God, in the Person of Jesus Christ, loved us; that is, he loved so much, *right to the end*, to the point of *giving his life for love*. For this is the meaning of the author of the fourth Gospel, the disciple whom Jesus loved, a meaning he makes explicit in his first letter:
"Think of the love that the Father has lavished on us, by letting us be called God's children; and that is what we are. Since God has loved us so much, we too should love one another. Anyone who fails to love can never have known God, because God is love" (1 Jn 3:1; 4:11, 8).

Think of the love that the Father has lavished on us.... See, contemplate the image of the newborn Jesus in the manger! As well as the *lectio divina* of our *Evangelium in nuce*, the vision through faith and love of our *Deus in praesepio*, "God in a manger," makes manifest and summarizes the totality of the great mystery of the Incarnation. It is perfectly appropriate to specify this vision "through faith and love." For, indeed, it is not enough for us to bow down before the Infant Jesus, recognizing in faith that—a fact unheard of in human history—this Child is "adorable" in the true sense of the word; *we must also love one another....* For the commandment of Love has been given us not only as a rule of life, but also as the sole infallible and universal means of recognizing and loving our God come to dwell among us, a man like us in all things. To have loved in truth and deed all those whom the Father places in our path through life is most assuredly to have known and loved him whom God made one of us, to have known and loved God in his humanity. If Herod, the scribes, the Pharisees, and the priests had loved the man Jesus, they would not have had such a mortal hatred of their incarnate God: *Whoever is without love does not know God....*

The unthinkable reality of the Incarnation did not take place in a stable in Bethlehem, but rather in Nazareth, in the most intimate and most secret manner there could be, in the womb of the Blessed Virgin Mary. The Feast of the Nativity of the Lord, whose splendors this volume celebrates, is the joyous remembrance of the day on which this event, until then hidden, was made manifest to the world. And this Infant-God in his epiphany, here he is, learning to speak, to walk, to read and write. Here he is in obedient submission to his parents. Here he is working, resting, enjoying himself. Here he is, setting off on the roads of the world, teaching, healing, remitting sins. Here he is, persecuted, suffering his Passion, loving those who are his own in the world, and loving them to the end. Here he is, dying in the Eucharist of his life for the salvation of the world. But here he is, rising from the dead, the firstborn of a multitude of brothers and sisters. Here he is, making all men of good will—saved through faith and the sacraments, and sanctified for ever through the practice of the new commandment— members of his Body. For this epiphany of the Son of the Savior God, inaugurated at Christmas, will continue to spread in human history through the gift of the Holy Spirit following his glorious Ascension, until the newborn God in the manger comes again in glory to judge the living and the dead. Then his divinity as well as his humanity will be fully and triumphantly manifested. In this final apotheosis, in which all the splendors of the feast of Christmas will participate, may the Son of Man turn toward me, toward you, and say to us: *"Come, you whom my Father has blessed, take for your heritage the kingdom prepared for you since the foundation of the world, for my Father placed me in the path of your life, and you loved me"* (cf. Mt 25:31-46).

Pierre-Marie Dumont

COMMENTARIES ON TWO-PAGE ARTWORK

Pages 8-9: **Hans Holbein the Younger** (1497–1543), *The Allegory of the Old and New Testaments* (early 1530s), oil on wood, 189.4 x 162.8 x 14.4 in.

In the center, a male nude—humanity—is seated at the base of a tree, the veritable axis of the composition. On the stone, a Latin inscription explains his unhappy pose: "What a miserable man am I! Who will deliver me from this body condemned to death through sin?" He is framed by two prophets pointing to the scenes in the right background: on the left, Isaiah indicates the Virgin Mary, whom we see kneeling on the summit of Mount Zion, illustrating his prophecy, *The virgin shall bear a son* (cf. Is 7:14). On the right, John the Baptist points to Jesus in the distance, as we read his famous words, *"Behold, the Lamb of God, who takes away the sin of the world"* (cf. Jn 1:29). Beneath the dramatic backdrop of a somber sky, the scenes on the left evoke sin and its consequences. In the foreground lies death in the form of an entombed skeleton. The sin of Adam and Eve is recalled in the fruit of the tree of knowledge and the presence of the serpent. Behind them rises Mount Sinai (counterbalancing Mount Zion) with, at its summit, the figure of Moses receiving the tablets of the law. Two further scenes make reference to Moses: the manna descending from the sky and the bronze serpent raised up as a result of the incredulity of the people. Facing this on the right, behind the crucifixion and the risen Christ crushing death underfoot as he leaves the tomb, the Annunciation to Mary and the proclamation to the shepherds are presented in soft light and serene colors.

Like a play of mirrors in which the central tree, with its dead branches on the left and foliage on the right, accentuates opposites, this panel is a splendid catechesis illustrating, among others, the verse from the Gospel of John: *"Though the law was given through Moses, grace and truth have come through Jesus Christ"* (Jn 1:17). Holbein develops this theological discourse and magnificently introduces us into the mystery of Christmas. For, if the law was the means of walking with God in the covenant established with Moses, it is grace that allows us to walk with God in the new covenant in Jesus Christ.

Pages 12-13: **Constantin Flavitski** (1830–1866), *Joseph Sold by His Brothers* (1855), oil on canvas, 23.2 x 29.7 in.

We witness here the abject bartering. The son of Jacob and Rachel, Joseph is his father's favorite child. His jealous brothers sell him as a slave, and he will be carried off to Egypt. The caravan of Ishmaelites has just arrived, *"their camels laden with gum, balm and resin to be taken down to Egypt"* (cf. Gn 37:25). Negotiations take place on the left side of the canvas, next to the cistern into which Joseph's brothers had thrown him, and from which he has just been pulled by Midianites. His fate is now sealed: while one merchant avidly holds out his hand for the twenty pieces of silver, his face marked by greed, the imposing figure of another member of the caravan, in the center, directs the mounting of the young man onto the camel that will carry him away.

Since the second century, a Christological interpretation has predominated in exegetical literature and homilies: Joseph is betrayed by his brothers just as Jesus is by Judas. He is taken to Egypt, like the Child Jesus in the flight into Egypt. Joseph's success with Pharaoh also prefigures Christ, the Savior of the world. In light of these facts, we cannot but be struck by this image of Joseph grabbed by the merchants, like Christ, his arms spread wide, being taken down from the cross. A tragic figure in this scene of Oriental aromas, facial features, and costumes that transports us a thousand miles away from our everyday life, this Joseph seems, for Flavitzky, to herald the One who will rise victorious from the tomb.

Pages 18-19: **Hans Holbein the Elder** (1465–1524), *The Tree of Jesse and the Genealogical Tree of the Dominican Order* (1501), closed exterior panels of an altarpiece, tempera and oil on wood.

What an astonishing composition in these two closed panels of the altarpiece of the Dominican church in Frankfurt: the tree of Jesse is represented facing the genealogical tree of the Dominican Order. The latter panel presents the principal thinkers, theologians, and religious who enriched the sanctity of the Order of Preachers, while the first retraces the lineage of Joseph, the father of Jesus, the *son of David* (Mt 1:1). This figured tree is inspired by the pronouncement of Isaiah: *"A shoot springs from the stock of Jesse, a scion thrusts from his roots. That day, the root of Jesse shall stand as a signal to the peoples. It will be sought out by the nations and its home will be glorious"* (Is 11:1, 10). Faithful to the biblical text, Holbein the Elder initiates this lineage with Jesse himself, depicted in the lower left, followed by the kings of Judah, Josiah, Ahaz, Hezekiah, and Manasseh; David and Solomon, kings of Israel; the patriarchs Isaac, Abraham, and Jacob; with the Virgin and Child culminating the genealogy in the upper register.

Through a simplicity of line that in no way hinders the precision of the portrayal, the artist harmoniously arranges the diverse and individualized portraits of these figures who made possible the coming of the One whom all await. As our eye follows the elegant tendrils supporting these busts, we recall that the Savior took flesh at the heart of this human lineage full of hope and thanksgiving.

Pages 34-35: **Fritz von Uhde** (1848–1911), *The Hard Path* or *The Road to Bethlehem* (c. 1890), oil on canvas, 46 x 49.6 in.

In 1863, Renan's *Life of Jesus* was published. In it, the author approaches the biography of Jesus just as he would that of any other man. Uhde, like so many others, was deeply affected by the work. His contemporary transposition of scenes from the Bible witness to a faith that looks to the moral practice of religion, depicting the "real people of God." From the outset, we are entered into the heart of the nineteenth century, as we follow a few steps behind this young couple of humble estate. There is still a long road ahead to Bethlehem. We feel the bitter chill of the fog into which the perspective line of this straight muddy path disappears. Emerging from the mist, a few cottages and the outline of large denuded trees seem to slumber behind a diaphanous curtain. It is winter. Only one feeble light testifies to any human presence. This couple is profoundly united in their solitude. Exhausted and slightly swaying, the young woman leans her weight on her husband's shoulder, on the point of dropping her pitiful baggage. With resolution and tenderness, he supports her arm and leans his face toward hers. Without even seeing their expressions, we seem to hear Joseph's words of encouragement and guess the silent acquiescence of the Virgin. For this indeed is Mary and Joseph on their journey to the city of David in answer to the call of the Lord, enduring, in their first pilgrimage as a married couple, all the harshness of the human condition into which their divine Child will come to share and redeem.

Pages 44-45: *The Nativity* (c. 1200), detail of the central panel of the altarpiece of Santa Maria d'Avià, Spain, tempera on poplar wood, 42.1 x 69.7 x 3 in.

The dark background of this composition is a tangible expression that the coming of the Son of God on earth is not really of this world, nor is it totally of the heavens. This space is the link between the two. The medieval artist is here still influenced by the canons of Byzantine representations. Following eastern tradition, the Virgin is lying down, resting after the delivery of her Child. The cavern represents the mysterious space of birth. Also an eastern legacy, the large mandorla surrounding her is the sign of majesty. It is doubtless for the same reason that the painter, with touching and pleasantly naïve attentiveness, supports Mary's head and feet with a cushion. He does the same for the newly born Jesus. The infant is wrapped in swaddling clothes and lies in a manger reminiscent of a sarcophagus, a tomb: for the seeds of Easter are already present in the birth of Christ. His body enveloped in cloths and bindings prefigures the shroud that will cover his battered corpse and become the clear evidence of his Resurrection. No more than a babe, his open eyes look toward heaven, to his Father, in the manner that will be his throughout his life in prayer. Slightly removed, a pensive Joseph stares at the Child and his mother. Perhaps he is meditating upon his mission. Finally, a familiar detail, the kindly presence of the donkey and the ox. For, according to the prophet, *"The ox knows its owner and the ass its master's crib, Israel knows nothing, my people understands nothing"* (Is 1:3). Like them, let us not be among those who fear to approach the Savior!

Pages 60-61: **Otto Dix** (1891–1969), *The Proclamation to the Shepherds on the Mount of Giants* (1942), mixed media on wood, 41.3 x 33 in.

A painter above all known as a representative of the "New Objectivity," the Neue Sachlichkeit, Dix was drawn to past masters such as Dürer and Cranach, Grünewald and Baldung Grien.
In this panel, Dix seems attached to careful observation of nature, and retains in his rapid brushwork, captured from life as observed on location, the ephemeral nature of the scene before our eyes. All this opens the way to a narrative world in which we join the two shepherds, astonished by this whirlwind of light erupting into sleeping nature. A host of swirling angels, immersed in miraculous clarity, accompanies the celestial messenger standing on a cloud, his hand raised to underscore the wondrous tidings he proclaims to the guardians of the flock: *"Do not be afraid. Listen, I bring you news of great joy, a joy to be shared by the whole people. Today in the town of David a savior has been born to you; he is Christ the Lord"* (Lk 2:10-11). The shepherds are not alone in their astonishment. Their dog and several of the sheep and lambs of the flock raise their heads attentively

to hear the divine message. Might the artist be borrowing the classical evocation of Christian disciples of Jesus in the form of sheep?

Along with the shepherds, let us follow Lamennais' invitation to: "Enter in advance into that eternity which you must one day inhabit." For he whom the shepherds will go to adore is for each one of us *"the good shepherd...who lays down his life for his sheep"* (Jn 10:11).

Pages 64-65: **Caspar David Friedrich** (1774–1840), *The Ages of Life* (c. 1826), page 7: "Two Angels in Prayer," pencil and sepia ink, 7.3 x 10.5 in.

What are these two angels looking at? A fine representative of German Romanticism, Friedrich enters into our imagination, translating it with intensity and simplicity.

The angels dwell close to God; the Bible even calls them *sons of God* (Ps 29:1). And indeed, it is the divine light that envelops them, that gilds their silhouettes and joined hands with a supernatural brilliance. They lean down in concert toward our earth, their gaze seeming to pierce through the clouds. Are these guardian angels, or those that take part in the earthly liturgy, uniting it, according to Revelation, with the celestial liturgy in which the elect join the angels to sing a new canticle, the song of the Lamb (cf. Rv 5:9-14; 15:3-4)? Perhaps they are contemplating the newborn in the manger, as Luke recounts: *"And suddenly with the angel there was a great throng of the heavenly host, praising God and singing: 'Glory to God in the highest heaven, and peace to men who enjoy his favor'"* (Lk 2:13-14). From the vantage point of this cottony skyscape, we can join our voices to the heavenly choir and, as the Eucharistic Prefaces invite us, "concelebrate" with them. Let us add our voices to their hymn of praise as we sing and proclaim: "Holy, Holy, Holy Lord God of hosts."

Pages 74-75: **Gustave Doré** (1832–1883), *The Star of the Magi* (1865), engraving of one of 230 Bible drawings.

As we contemplate this engraving, we seem to hear Maurice Jarre's majestic theme music to Lawrence of Arabia ringing in our ears…. Yet the imaginary vision of Gustave Doré helps us forget our prosaic clichés of the Orient. Our gaze, like the Magi, voyages. Having circled the ring of members in this imposing caravan, our eyes are then drawn to the hieratic figure surmounting all from his perch on a camel with disproportionately large hooves, before our glance, running ahead of this voyaging cohort, loses itself on the horizon, and comes to halt on the brilliant star. The star is the sole source of illumination, its rays revealing the figures in stunning relief. They caress the faces and cast gossamer shadows on the ground, creating an otherwordly, almost ghostly sensation. Such iconography cannot help but strike the imagination, recalling the words of Isaiah: *"The nations come to your light and kings to your dawning brightness"* (Is 60:3).

"Then, Balthazar, Melchior, Caspar, Magi Kings,/ Laden with vases where enamels glow,/ Vermeil and silver, with their camels go,/ As in the bodied, old imaginings." Doré outstrips this poem by José Maria de Hérédia through his evocative power, misunderstood in his day, which carries us to the frontiers of the sublime and an encounter with the One who shines out in the heart of our darkness.

Page 79: *The Star of Balaam* (c. 350), Catacombs of Saint Thecla, Rome, fresco, 27.5 x 26.7 in.

Balaam was a pagan prophet from the banks of the Euphrates whom Moab asked to curse Israel. He ordered the seer to proclaim the pre-battle oracles favorable, foretelling ultimate victory. But Balaam is constrained by some irresistible force to speak the words in his heart, in which he affirms that *"a star from Jacob takes the leadership, a scepter arises from Israel"* (Nm 24:17). The promise of divine power still lies hidden. It is the promise of the rising star, of the coming of the Messiah. The effectiveness and restraint of this depiction adds to the modernity of the fresco. In rapid, assured strokes, the image stands out against the stucco, thanks to the ochre surfaces and the elegant, almost dancing forms. The seer turns his back to us, pointing out the star with a lively gesture to his companion. The latter, with a natural, familiar gesture, shades his eyes with his right hand, as though to get a better look at the shining star. The artist implicates the viewer in the scene, making him a further beneficiary of the prophecy. Let us not forget that this fresco adorns a burial place. We can thus understand this oracle as an encouragement to believe that the power of Christ will be wielded for the redemption of the world.

Pages 92-93: **Edwin Longsden Long** (1829–1891), *Anno Domini*, or *The Long Journey in Egypt* (1883), oil on canvas, 96 x 192 in.

The prophet Hosea had proclaimed: *"I called my son out of Egypt"* (Hos 11:1). And here, the greater part of the journey is over. Jesus, Mary, and Joseph arrive in a foreign land, in the midst of a crowd indifferent to their presence. Two processions cross paths. In the foreground, a young girl calls out to the humble cortège of the Holy Family, proffering them a little statuette while, in the background, a musician fixes her gaze upon them. Most of the figures are taking part in a much larger cortège. Is it a funeral? For a young woman is lying on a stretcher surrounded by three men bending over her, while a group on their knees bows, their arms outstretched toward the statue of a goddess. This golden statue is Isis, who holds on her lap the Pharaoh, wearing the Hedjet, the white crown of Upper Egypt. A group of sacred musicians precedes the statue. In addition to the tambourines and the flutes, we recognize the sistrum, played for dances and religious ceremonies. The insignia bearing an ankh (also called the cross of life) and the figures of the gods Horus and Thot firmly anchor this scene in ancient Egyptian culture, as do the canopic jars, incense burners, and fans. Following a trip in 1874 that took him to Egypt and Syria, Long began painting oriental scenes. Here he gives proof of a true archeologist's eye in the minute details of the objects and costumes, not to mention the depiction of a temple reminiscent of Luxor: we can see one of its towers, the colossal statue, and the great pillared hall. But this canvas is not just a pretext to pander to the "Egyptomania" in vogue in the nineteenth century. The juxtaposition of the two religious groups is an affirmation of the humble presence of the true God in the midst of a pagan culture doomed to destruction. *"See! Yahweh, riding a swift cloud, comes to Egypt. The idols of Egypt tremble before him, and the hearts of the Egyptians sink within them"* (Is 19:1).

Pages 98-99: **Léon Cogniet** (1794–1880), *Scene from the Massacre of the Innocents* (1824), oil on canvas, 104.3 x 92.5 in.

Here is an unforgettable face. A face in which terror rivals with incomprehension and a plea for help. This woman is not alone in expressing the horror of the scene, for we read in the eyes of her child all the intensity of the nightmare the people of Bethlehem experience here.

Through an economy of means to set the scene—which in no way detracts from the clever framing and the intensity of the quasi-photographic image—the painter, a contemporary of Delacroix and Géricault, plunges us into the indescribable chaos caused by Herod's order for a manhunt. We can almost hear the cry of horror and despair, of which the prophet Jeremiah spoke: *"A voice was heard in Ramah, sobbing and loudly lamenting: it was Rachel weeping for her children, refusing to be comforted because they were no more"* (Mt 2:18).

We are far from the sweetness of Christmas night. Along with this mother, we plunge into a night of anguish, crouched in this dark corner echoing with the footsteps of another mother racing down the steps, the cries of pursuit, and the clashes we spy in the distance. We too are assaulted by the edge of this crumbling wall that aggresses the eye and, in its stunning foreshortening, adds depth and a poignant realism to the composition. Will this maternal hand firmly stifling the cries of her beloved child be enough to escape the murderous madness? Let us think of all mothers who, across time and borders, manifest in their souls and in their flesh this love that likens them to God.

Page 105: **Desiderio da Settignano** (c. 1428–1464), *Jesus Christ and Saint John the Baptist as Children*, marble, 19.7 in. diameter.

Two smiling children, happy to be together. Up until the very end of the fifteenth century, this theme of Jesus and John the Baptist as children—often represented in European art—was still almost exclusively the domain of Florentine art.

The Gospels do not mention any encounter between the Child Jesus and the young John the Baptist. It was the lives of the saints, written in the medieval period, that provided the source of inspiration: the Baptist was said to have visited Christ at the moment of the Nativity, and then again during the return of the Holy Family from Egypt, at a time when he had already developed a precocious taste for withdrawing to the desert and had adopted his clothing of camel skin.

This representation is probably an evocation of the second encounter. Christ, on the left, is distinguished from his slightly older cousin by the cross superimposed on his halo. He lays his right hand on John the Baptist's camel-skin tunic, as though attesting to the importance of this stage in the development of John as a prophet. It is a bit like an anticipation of Jesus' portrait of the Precursor: *"I tell you solemnly, of all the children born of women, a greater than John the Baptist has never been seen; yet the least in the kingdom of heaven is greater than he is"* (Mt 11:11).

The circular form of the tondo perfectly suits this intimate scene, enhancing the unity and focus of the composition. The two faces, open-mouthed and with raised eyebrows, are transfigured. The joy of Christ's face and the fervent respect in John the Baptist's shy features witness to a spontaneous relationship, without detracting from the dimension of veneration appropriate to the supernatural import of this iconographic theme.

Pages 106-107: **Jacob Jordaens** (1593–1678), *The Holy Family with Saint John the Baptist* (c. 1620–1625), detail, oil on wood, 48.4 x 37 in.

While Jordaens is known as a painter of scenes of daily life, we should not forget his brilliant and prolific career as a religious painter. His taste for daily life can be found here, in this family portrait he offers to the viewer's eye. The heavy, rich drapery of blue-tinged velvet enhances this group of figures. Here is a family like any other. The young mother and her companion, in the prime of life, are happy, not to say proud, to present their charming chubby-cheeked toddler to us, with his glowing little face and hair the color of sunshine.

The strong light coming from the left places in relief these faces with naturalistic features and smooth complexions. Mary stares intently at us, her lips parted as if to speak to us. The handsome serene face of Joseph betrays deep reflection, underscored by the familiar gesture of his hand stroking his beard.

What parent doesn't recall the blessed moment of the arrival of their child? Who among us cannot share in the joy and the awakening consciousness of Mary and Joseph's mission? Like every father and every mother, they have to take on an unfathomable responsibility. But for these parents, it goes well beyond the simply human dimension; it is universal. Thanks to them, *"Jesus increased in wisdom, in stature, and in favor with God and men"* (Lk 2:52).

ART CREDITS

HYMN CREDITS

O nimis felix, O more than blessed; from Ut queant laxis, attr. Paulus Diaconus, 8th cent., tr. M.J. Blacker and G.H. Palmer, c. 1905. Public domain.

Inclitos Christi, Singing, we laurel Christ's heroic servants; author unknown, 20th cent, tr. Kathleen Pluth, 2014. Used with permission.

Te Ioseph celebrent, Joseph! to thee by hosts on high; Juan Escollar, 17th cent.; tr. R. F. Littledale,19th cent. Public domain.

Verbum salutis omnium, The Savior of all men, the Word; anon., 5th-6th cent.; tr. Dylan Schrader, 2009. Used with permission.

Magnis prophetae vocibus, The prophets with how great a voice; anon., 10th cent.; tr. Michael Church, 2011. Public domain.

A solis ortus cardine, From east to west, from shore to shore; Coelius Sedulius, 5th cent.; tr. John Ellerton, 1826-1893. Public domain.

Tibi, Christe, Thee, O Christ, the Father's splendor; Rabanus Maurus, 776-856; tr. John M. Neale, 1851. Public domain.

Vox clara ecce intonat, Hark! a herald voice is calling; anon., 6th century; tr. Edward Caswall, 1906. Public domain.

Quicumque Christum quaeritis, All you who seek the gentle Christ; Aurelius Clemens Prudentius, 348-413; tr. © Benedictine Nuns of the Abbey of St. Cecilia, Ryde, Isle of Wight, UK. Used with permission.

Hostis Herodes impie, Why should the wicked Herod fear; Aurelius Clemens Prudentius, 348-413; tr. © Benedictine Nuns of the Abbey of St. Cecilia, Ryde, Isle of Wight, UK. Used with permission.

Quis iste tantus, "What is this marvelous thing," they say; from Hostis Herodes impie, Aurelius Clemens Prudentius, 348-413; tr. © Benedictine Nuns of the Abbey of St. Cecilia, Ryde, Isle of Wight, UK. Used with permission.

Audit tyrannus anxius, The anxious tyrant's troubled ears; from Quicumque Christum quaeritis, Aurelius Clemens Prudentius, 348-413; tr. © Benedictine Nuns of the Abbey of St. Cecilia, Ryde, Isle of Wight, UK. Used with permission.

Salvete flores martyrum, Hail, fairest flow'rs of martyrdom; from Quicumque Christum quaeritis, Aurelius Clemens Prudentius, 348-413; tr. © Benedictine Nuns of the Abbey of St. Cecilia, Ryde, Isle of Wight, UK. Used with permission.

O lux beata caelitum, O Jesus, light of heaven's joy; Aurelius Clemens Prudentius, 348-413; tr. © Benedictine Nuns of the Abbey of St. Cecilia, Ryde, Isle of Wight, UK. Used with permission.

Christe, splendor Patris, Splendor of the Father; author unknown; tr. © Benedictine Nuns of the Abbey of St. Cecilia, Ryde, Isle of Wight, UK. Used with permission.

Back cover: **Rosso Fiorentino** (1494–1541), *Musician Angel*, oil on wood,
18.5 x 15.3 in.

Did you recognize this little angel concentrating on his lute-playing? If you've ever had the occasion to visit Florence, you will have come across him in one of the rooms in the Uffizi Gallery. Nothing, not even your presence or your tender gaze, would have disturbed his absorption in accompanying the song Creation sings to the Lord from all eternity. This figure, a witness to the influence of the *putti* of antiquity, is one of a long line of musician angels that appeared in twelfth-century iconographic representations based on biblical texts and commentaries by the Church Fathers. Here, we are far from those great gatherings where angelic orchestras set the scene. This youthful being has the privilege of contemplating the divinity "solo" (as indicated by the scarlet tinge to his wings). We might even imagine a rehearsal in which he is intent on positioning his little fingers to strike a perfect note, worthy of the One who is the source of all beauty.

As we listen and attune ourselves to the harmony of the ineffable, may our gaze join his in this touching and exquisite rendition. And, as we close this book, may we, as the Eucharistic Liturgy invites us, unite ourselves with these angels who celebrate the greatness of God, and join our voices to their hymn of praise as we sing and proclaim: "Holy, Holy, Holy Lord!"

Printed in September 2014 by Transcontinental, Canada
Edition number: MGN 14018
www.magnificat.com